THE YEAR YOU WERE BORN
1941

A fascinating book about the year 1941 with information on:
Events of the year UK, Adverts of 1941, Cost of living, Births, Sporting events,
Book publications, Movies, Music, World events and People in power.

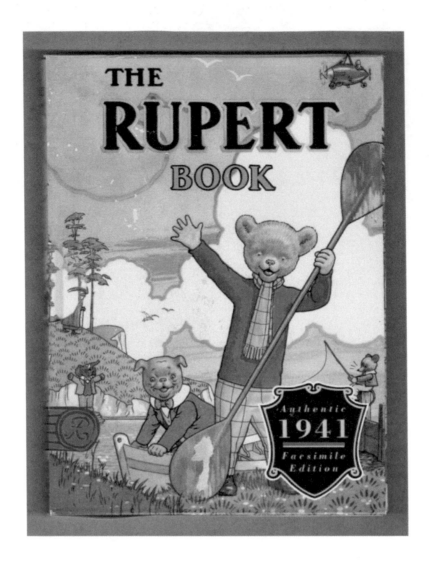

INDEX

January

1st Royal Air Force Llandwrog or, more simply, RAF Llandwrog is a former Royal Air Force station located at Llandwrog, southwest of Caernarfon, Gwynedd, Wales. The site opened in the 1st January 1941 as a RAF Bomber Command airfield for training gunners, radio operators and navigators and closed after the end of the Second World War in 1945. It reopened in 1969 and remains in civil operation today as Caernarfon Airport.

2nd The Cardiff Blitz. Over 100 bombers attacked the city over a 10-hour period beginning at 6.37 PM on the night of 2nd January 1941. Dropping high explosive bombs, incendiary bombs and parachute mines, the Riverside area was the first to be bombed. In Grangetown, the Hollyman Brothers bakery was hit by a parachute mine and 32 people who were using the basement as a shelter were killed. When the raid was over 165 people had been killed and 427 more injured, while nearly 350 homes were destroyed or had to be demolished.

9th The Avro Manchester Mark III BT308, prototype of the Avro Lancaster heavy bomber, first flies, from RAF Ringway

January

17th A German Heinkel He 111 meteorological aircraft is crash-landed on Fair Isle.

19th World War II: British troops attack Italian-held Eritrea.

20th Fire watching became mandatory for business premises, to limit incendiary damage.

21st The Daily Worker, newspaper of the Communist Party of Great Britain, is suppressed by the (Labour) Home Secretary in the Churchill war ministry, Herbert Morrison (until September 1942) in view of its continuing pro-Soviet stance.

22nd Battle of Tobruk: Australian and British forces attack and capture Tobruk (Libya) from the Italians.

January

31st | On the 31st January 1941, Josef Jakobs was flown from Schiphol Airport in the Netherlands to Ramsey in Huntingdonshire. He parachuted from the aircraft and landed in a field near Dove House Farm, but broke his ankle during the process. The following morning, Jakobs attracted the attention of two farmers, Charles Baldock and Harry Coulson, by firing his pistol into the air. Baldock and Coulson notified members of the local Home Guard, who quickly apprehended Jakobs. He was caught still wearing his flying suit and carrying £500 in British currency, forged identity papers, a radio transmitter, and a German sausage. Josef Jakobs was a German spy and the last person to be executed at the Tower of London. He was captured shortly after parachuting into the United Kingdom during the Second World War. Convicted of espionage under the Treachery Act 1940, Jakobs was shot by a military firing squad. He was not hanged because he was captured as an enemy combatant.

February

5th | On the 5th February 1941, the Air Training Corps (ATC) was officially established, with King George VI agreeing to be the Air Commodore-in-Chief, and issuing a Royal Warrant setting out the Corps' aims. Within the first month of its existence, the size of the old ADCC, now the ATC, virtually doubled to more than 400 squadrons and continued to grow thereafter. A new badge was designed for the ATC and, once approved by the King, was distributed in August 1941. The motto ' Venture Adventure ', devised by Air Commodore Chamier, was adopted by the ATC and incorporated into the badge.

11th | RMS Queen Elizabeth begins her first voyage as a troopship, from Singapore.

12th | Reserve Constable Albert Alexander, a patient at the Radcliffe Infirmary in Oxford, becomes the first person treated with penicillin intravenously, by Howard Florey's team. He reacts positively but there is insufficient supply of the drug to reverse his terminal infection. A successful treatment is achieved during May.

February

12th | Tom Johnston is appointed Secretary of State for Scotland, a post which he holds until the end of the wartime coalition.

13th | Opening of RAF Valley on Anglesey as a Fighter Command station.

14th | Six people are killed in an air raid on Port Talbot.

19th | The Swansea Blitz was the heavy and sustained bombing of Swansea by the German Luftwaffe from the 19th to 21st February 1941. A total of 230 people were killed and 397 were injured. Swansea was selected by the Germans as a legitimate strategic target due to its importance as a port and docks and the oil refinery just beyond, and its destruction was key to Nazi German war efforts as part of their strategic bombing campaign aimed at crippling coal export and demoralising civilians and emergency services.

February

21st | First flight by a Royal Air Force flying boat through the "Donegal Corridor", neutral Republic of Ireland airspace between its base in Northern Ireland and the Atlantic Ocean, a concession secretly agreed by Éamon de Valera.

24th | SS Jonathan Holt is torpedoed in a convoy off Cape Wrath by German submarine U-97 with the loss of 51 of her 57 crew, including English travel writer Robert Byron.

26th | Four people are killed in an air raid on Cardiff. Buildings damaged include Cardiff University and children's home.

March

2nd | John Gilbert Winant takes up post as United States Ambassador to the United Kingdom in succession to Joseph P. Kennedy; he will serve for 5 years.

March

11th	President Franklin D. Roosevelt signs the Lend-Lease Act into United States law, allowing the country to supply military equipment to Britain.

Luftwaffe air raids on Manchester cause extensive damage to the city, a notable casualty being Old Trafford football stadium, home of Manchester United, which is severely damaged. |
| 13th | As a result of the raids on the nights of the13th and 14th March 1941, the town was largely destroyed and it suffered the worst destruction and civilian loss of life in all of Scotland. 1,200 people died, 1,000 people were seriously injured, and hundreds more were injured by blast debris. Out of approximately 12,000 houses, only eight remained undamaged — with 4,000 completely destroyed and 4,500 severely damaged. Over 35,000 people were made homeless. |

March

15th | The Plymouth Blitz was a series of bombing raids carried out by the Nazi German Luftwaffe on the English city of Plymouth in the Second World War from the 15th March. The royal dockyards at HMNB Devonport were the main target in order to facilitate Nazi German efforts during the Battle of the Atlantic. Portsmouth, some 170 miles away in Hampshire, was also targeted by the Luftwaffe due to the presence of a royal dockyard there.

21st | The coaster Millisle is sunk by German planes off Caldey Island, killing 10 crew members.

25th | On the 25th March 1941 the Faraday and four other ships set sail from Falmouth bound for Milford Haven. The ships became separated in poor visibility and about 7:45 p.m. the Faraday was attacked by a Heinkel He 111 which strafed and bombed the ship, killing eight and wounding 25 of the crew, and caused a major fire in the oil bunkers forcing the crew to abandon ship. The aircraft was itself shot down by the ship's crew. She later ran aground off St. Anne's Head. The cable was recovered, however the wreck of the Faraday still lies in shallow waters and is a popular attraction for divers.

27th | The Battle of Cape Matapan. In the 27th March 1941, as British ships of the Mediterranean Fleet covered troop movements to Greece, Mavis Batey, a cryptographer at Bletchley Park, made a breakthrough, reading the Italian naval Enigma for the first time. The first message, the cryptic "Today's the day minus three," was followed three days later by a second message reporting the sailing of an Italian battle fleet comprising one battleship, six heavy and two light cruisers, plus destroyers to attack the merchant convoys supplying British forces. As always with Enigma, the intelligence breakthrough was concealed from the Italians by ensuring there was a plausible reason for the Allies to have detected and intercepted their fleet. In this case, it was a carefully directed reconnaissance plane.

31st | Three people are killed in air raids on Swansea.

April

7th | The Belfast Blitz: The first was on the night of 7–8 April 1941, a small attack which probably took place only to test Belfast's defences. The next took place on Easter Tuesday, 15th April 1941. Two hundred bombers of the Luftwaffe attacked military and manufacturing targets in the city of Belfast. Some 900 people died as a result of the bombing and 1,500 were injured. High explosive bombs predominated in this raid. Apart from those on London, this was the greatest loss of life in any night raid during the Blitz.

April

15th	The Belfast blitz: 1,000 people are killed in bombing raids on Belfast. 71 firemen with 13 fire tenders from Dundalk, Drogheda, Dublin, and Dún Laoghaire cross the Irish border to assist their Belfast colleagues.
18th	Heaviest air-raid of the year on London.

April

21st	Greece capitulates. British troops withdraw to Crete.
29th	26 people are killed in air raids aimed at coal mines in the Rhondda, and a further seven in Cardiff.

May

2nd	the 'May Week Raids'; sustained heavy bombing on Merseyside result in over 1,700 deaths and well over 1,000 injuries.
6th	The attack began around midnight on the 6th May when around 350 German bombers attacked the town. Bombs fell all over the town and surrounding area; serious damage being inflicted on East Crawford Street and Belville Street. Many civilians fled to the tunnels in the east end of the town, significantly reducing casualties the next night

May

7th Air raid sirens at 12:15am on the 7th May marked the beginning of a second night of bombing. Initially, incendiary bombs were dropped around the perimeter of the town. The second wave attacked primarily the east end and centre of Greenock; the distillery in Ingleston Street had been set alight in the first wave, causing a huge fire which acted as a beacon for the rest of the bomber force. The final wave came around 2am; dropping high explosive bombs and parachute land mines which caused widespread destruction. At 3:30am the "All Clear" sounded but a large area of the town was in flames. The sugar refineries, distillery and foundries were all extensively damaged, the Municipal Buildings complex was partly destroyed, and several churches were left as burnt out shells. However, damage to the shipyards was minimal.

8th The German submarine U-110 is captured by the Royal Navy in the North Atlantic with its Enigma cryptography machine and codebooks intact. Picture below of HMS Bulldog capturing U-110.

May

10th The House of Commons is damaged by the Luftwaffe in an air raid.

Rudolf Hess parachutes into Scotland claiming to be on a peace mission.

12th The Honours of Scotland are secretly buried within Edinburgh Castle as a precaution against invasion.

15th The first British jet aircraft, the Gloster E.28/39, is flown at RAF Cranwell in Lincolnshire. The E.28/39 was the product of a specification which had been issued by the Air Ministry for a suitable aircraft to test the novel jet propulsion designs that Frank Whittle had been developing during the 1930s. Gloster and the company's chief designer, George Carter, worked with Whittle to develop an otherwise conventional aircraft fitted with a Power Jets W.1 turbojet engine. Flying for the first time on the 15th May 1941, a pair of E.28/39 aircraft was produced for the flight test programme. Following initial satisfactory reports, these aircraft continued to be flown to test increasingly refined engine designs and new aerodynamic features. Despite the loss of the second prototype, due to improper maintenance causing a critical aileron failure, the E.28/39 was considered to be a success.

17th Tipton, near Dudley in the midlands, is bombed by the Luftwaffe for the second time in six months, with a further six civilian deaths.

May

24th In the North Atlantic, the German battleship Bismarck sinks HMS Hood killing all but three crewmen on what was the pride of the Royal Navy.

Bismarck

HMS Hood

26th In the North Atlantic, Fairey Swordfish biplanes from the carrier HMS Ark Royal fatally cripple the German battleship Bismarck in torpedo attack.

"Operation David": Western Command stages an exercise involving 20,000 troops simulating an invasion landing between Porthcawl and Kidwelly and a "Battle of Pontardulais".

27th Speaking in the House of Commons of the United Kingdom, Prime Minister Winston Churchill rules out the introduction of conscription in the North.

June

1st A German Junkers 88 is shot down near Llandudno, killing four crew.

2nd 2 adults and 8 children are killed at Buckhaven when a naval mine explodes on the foreshore.

4th Britain invades Iraq, the pro-Axis government there is overthrown.

11th The Baron Carnegie, a cargo ship, is sunk by German planes off Strumble Head, killing 25 crew.

13th The ferry St Patrick is sunk by German planes off Strumble Head, killing thirty.

August

1st During World War II, the Political Warfare Executive (PWE) was a British clandestine body created to produce and disseminate both white and black propaganda, with the aim of damaging enemy morale and sustaining the morale of the Occupied countries. The Executive was formed on the 1st August 1941, reporting to the Foreign Office. The staff came mostly from SO1, which had been until then the propaganda arm of the Special Operations Executive. The organisation was governed by a committee initially comprising Anthony Eden, Brendan Bracken and Hugh Dalton, together with officials Rex Leeper, Dallas Brooks and Robert Bruce Lockhart as chairman.

August

9th — Franklin D. Roosevelt and Winston Churchill meet on board ship at Naval Station Argentia, Newfoundland. The Atlantic Charter (released 14 August), setting goals for post-war international cooperation, is agreed as a result.

RAF pilot Douglas Bader taken prisoner by the Germans after a mid-air collision over France.

12th — Dudley, which suffered 10 fatalities in a landmine attack in November last year, suffers five more fatalities when a second landmine is dropped in the town.

16th — HMS Mercury Royal Navy Signals School and Combined Signals School opens at Leydene, near Petersfield, Hampshire.

18th — The NFS was created on the 18th August 1941 by the amalgamation of the wartime national Auxiliary Fire Service (AFS) and the local authority fire brigades (about 1,600 of them). It existed until 1948, when it was again split by the Fire Services Act 1947, with fire services reverting to local authority control, although this time there were far fewer brigades, with only one per county and county borough. The NFS had full-time and part-time members, male and female. Its uniform was the traditional dark blue double-breasted tunic, and it adopted the peaked cap worn by the AFS instead of the peak less sailor-style cap which had been worn by many pre-war fire brigades (including the London Fire Brigade). The peaked cap was retained by fire services after the war. When they were on duty, but in the frequent long stretches between calls, many firemen and firewomen performed vital wartime manufacturing work, in workshops in the fire stations or adjacent to them. This was entirely voluntary, but since many of the wartime personnel had worked in factories before the war it was work with which they were familiar and skilled.

September

2nd | The Royal Air Force began daylight bombing of targets in northern France.

4th | The Greer incident occurred in the North Atlantic when the German submarine U-652 fired a torpedo at the American destroyer USS Greer, perhaps believing that the American ship had launched an attack that had actually come from a British bomber.

15th | The British passenger ship Empire Eland was torpedoed and sunk in the Atlantic Ocean by German submarine U-94.

17th | The British government ordered potatoes to be sold at 1d so people would eat more of them.

20th | The British ferry Portsdown struck a mine and sank in the Celtic Sea with the loss of 23 lives.

22nd | "Russian Tank Week" began in the United Kingdom. From this day through to the 26th September, all armoured vehicles produced in Britain were to be delivered to the Soviets.

25th | Convoy HG 73 came under attack in the North Atlantic. The British liner SS Avoceta was torpedoed and sunk by the German submarine U-203.

27th | British Commandos executed Operation Chopper, an overnight raid on Saint-Aubin-d'Arquenay in occupied France.

28th | The first British convoy of supplies for the Soviet Union departed Iceland for Arkhangelsk.

30th | Winston Churchill gave a speech in the House of Commons reviewing the war situation.

October

6th | The British cargo ship Thistlegorm was bombed and sunk in the Red Sea off Ras Muhammad by the Luftwaffe.

16th | The British corvette HMS Gladiolus was lost while escorting convoy SC 48. The cause of its loss is unknown.

18th | The British destroyer HMS Broadwater escorting convoy SC 48 was sunk south of Iceland by the German submarine U-101.

21st | The British gunboat HMS Gnat was torpedoed and damaged off Bardia by German submarine U-79. The Gnat would be towed and beached at Alexandria and be used as an anti-aircraft platform for the rest of the war.

22nd | The Royal Fleet Auxiliary oil tanker Darkdale was torpedoed and sunk at Jamestown, Saint Helena by the German submarine U-68.

23rd | The British destroyer HMS Cossack was torpedoed and damaged in the Atlantic Ocean by the German submarine U-563. The Cossack tried to return to Gibraltar for repairs but would sink in bad weather four days later.

November

1st   Announcement that radical politician Sir Charles Trevelyan is donating his family home, Wallington Hall, Northumberland, to the National Trust, it's first such stately home acquisition.

3rd   The British merchant ship Flynderborg was sunk off Newfoundland by German submarine U-202.

4th   Viscount Halifax was pelted with eggs and tomatoes by isolationist women demonstrators in Detroit as he was leaving City Hall. Halifax was afterwards quoted as saying, "How fortunate you Americans are, in Britain we get only one egg a week and we are glad of those." The quote was actually fabricated by someone in the British Press Service, but it was widely disseminated in the media and created a burst of sympathy and goodwill towards the British and Halifax in particular.

8th   The Battle of the Duisburg Convoy was fought over the night of November 8/9, ending in British victory.

10th   The British launched Operation Flipper, a commando raid on the headquarters of Erwin Rommel.

12th   King George VI opened a new session of British Parliament. "The developments of the past year have strengthened the resolution of my peoples and of my allies to prosecute this war against aggression until final victory," his speech from the throne began.

13th   The British aircraft carrier Ark Royal was torpedoed and severely damaged off Gibraltar by the German submarine U-81.

14th   The British cargo ship Empire Defender was torpedoed and sunk south of the Galite Islands, Tunisia by Italian aircraft.

18th   Operation Crusader was a military operation during the Second World War by the British Eighth Army with Allied contingents, against the Axis forces in North Africa commanded by Generalleutnant Erwin Rommel. The operation was intended to by-pass Axis defences on the Egyptian–Libyan frontier, defeat the Axis armoured forces and relieve the 1941 Siege of Tobruk.

On the 18th November 1941, the Eighth Army launched a surprise attack. The British armoured force became dispersed and suffered 530 tank losses against Axis losses of about 100 tanks up to 22nd November. On the 23rd November the 5th South African Brigade was destroyed at Sidi Rezegh, while inflicting many German tank casualties. On the 24th November Rommel ordered the "dash to the wire", causing chaos in the British rear echelons but allowing the British armoured forces to recover. On the 27th November the New Zealanders reached the Tobruk garrison, relieving the siege.

The battle continued into December, when supply shortages forced Rommel to narrow his front and shorten his lines of communication. On the 7th December 1941 Rommel withdrew the Axis forces to the Gazala position and on the 15th December ordered a withdrawal to El Agheila.

20th   The British cargo ship Empire Dorado collided with the Greek cargo ship Theomitor in the Atlantic Ocean. Empire Dorado was taken in tow by a Royal Navy ship but sank two days later.

21st   Arthur Cunningham ordered the British 70th Division to break out of its encirclement at Tobruk, which it managed to do after a hard day's fighting.

November

22nd   Operation Sunstar was a Second World War raid on Houlgate in Normandy, France over the night of 22/23 November 1941. British Commandos of No. 9 Commando took part in the raid their objective was the Batterie de Tournebride on the Butte de Houlgate. Ninety men of No.9 Commando travelled across the English Channel on HMS Prince Leopold and landed at the bottom of the Vaches Noires. The ship also transported four Assault Landing Craft which were used for the landing, four Motor Gun Boats were used to provide cover. The operation encountered difficulties and did not succeed in destroying the battery or taking any prisoners but they did obtain documents and other information.

23rd   The British 7th Armoured Division was forced to withdraw south of Sidi Rezegh after getting outflanked by Axis troops.

24th   The British light cruiser HMS Dunedin was torpedoed and sunk off Recife, Brazil by German submarine U-124.

25th   The British battleship HMS Barham was torpedoed and sunk off Alexandria by German submarine U-331 with the loss of more than 800 crew.

27th   The Siege of Tobruk ended in Allied victory when the besieged garrison was relieved by the British 8th Army.

December

5th   Britain declared war on Finland, Hungary and Romania.

6th   The British submarine HMS Perseus struck a mine and sank in the Ionian Sea off Cephalonia.

7th   Winston Churchill was dining at Chequers, the country house of the Prime Minister of the United Kingdom, with the American diplomats John Gilbert Winant and W. Averell Harriman when the news of the Pearl Harbour attack arrived. Churchill realized that the United States would now enter the war and that Britain would no longer have to fight alone. He later wrote of that night, "Being saturated and satiated with emotion and sensation, I went to bed and slept the sleep of the saved and thankful."

8th   The British House of Commons convened on short notice in light of recent events. Winston Churchill made a speech concluding, "We have at least four-fifths of the population of the globe upon our side. We are responsible for their safety and for their future. In the past we have had a light which flickered, in the present we have a light which flames, and in the future there will be a light which shines over all the land and sea."

9th   On the 9th December 1941 detachments from No. 6 and No. 12 Commandos, some Norwegian soldiers, took part in a raid on the town of Florø in Norway. Embarking on HMS Prince Charles, an infantry landing ship, they set out from Scapa Flow. During the voyage an incident occurred while some of the men were priming grenades for the raid which resulted in six men were killed and another 11 were seriously wounded, nevertheless the decision was made to continue with the raid. In the end, however, due to navigational difficulties the operation was eventually called off when the naval commander was unable to locate the fjord upon which Florø was located.

December

10th | The sinking of Prince of Wales and Repulse was a naval engagement in the Second World War, part of the war in the Pacific, that took place off the east coast of present-day Malaysia, which was then a British colony known as Malaya, near Kuantan, Pahang, where the Royal Navy battleship HMS Prince of Wales and battlecruiser HMS Repulse were sunk by land-based bombers and torpedo bombers of the Imperial Japanese Navy on the 10th December 1941. In Japanese, the engagement was referred to as the Naval Battle of Malaya.

HMS Prince of Wales

HMS Repulse

11th | The British destroyer HMS Jackal was damaged in the Mediterranean Sea by Italian torpedo bombers and knocked out of action until May 1942.

14th | The British light cruiser HMS Galatea was torpedoed and sunk off Alexandria by the German submarine U-557.

15th | The British 4th Armoured Brigade arrived at Bir Halegh el Eleba where they planned to outflank the Axis forces.

The British cargo ship Empire Barracuda was torpedoed and sunk in the Atlantic Ocean by the German submarine U-77.

18th | National Service (No. 2) Act comes into effect: All men and women aged 18–60 are now liable to some form of national service, including military service for men under 51 and unmarried women between 20 and 30. The first military registration of 18½-year-olds takes place. The schedule of reserved occupations is abandoned.

19th | The British light cruiser HMS Neptune struck naval mines off Tripoli and sank. The destroyer Kandahar struck a mine and was damaged trying to come to Neptune's rescue and had to be scuttled the next day.

The British destroyer Stanley was torpedoed and sunk in the Atlantic Ocean by German submarine U-574. The sloop HMS Stork then depth charged, rammed and sank U-574.

21st | The first play of the twelve-episode radio play cycle The Man Born to Be King, based on the life of Jesus, premiered on the BBC Home Service.

December

22nd Winston Churchill arrived in Washington, D.C. aboard HMS Duke of York after a secret ten-day journey across the Atlantic. The Arcadia Conference began.

26th Operation Anklet was the codename given to a British Commando raid during the Second World War. The raid on the Lofoten Islands was carried out on December 26th, 1941, by 300 men from No. 12 Commando and the Norwegian Independent Company 1. The landing party was supported by 22 ships from three navies. At the same time, another raid was taking place in Vågsøy. This raid was Operation Archery, on the 27th December 1941, and Operation Anklet was seen as a diversionary raid for this bigger raid, intended to draw away the German naval and air forces.

28th The British cargo ship Volo was torpedoed and sunk off the coast of Egypt by German submarine U-75. The destroyer HMS Kipling chased the U-boat down and sank U-75 with depth charges.

30th Winston Churchill made the "Chicken Speech" to Canadian Parliament. In reference to a comment made by Philippe Pétain that Britain would be invaded and "have its neck wrung like a chicken" by the Germans in three weeks, Churchill exclaimed, "Some chicken! Some neck!"

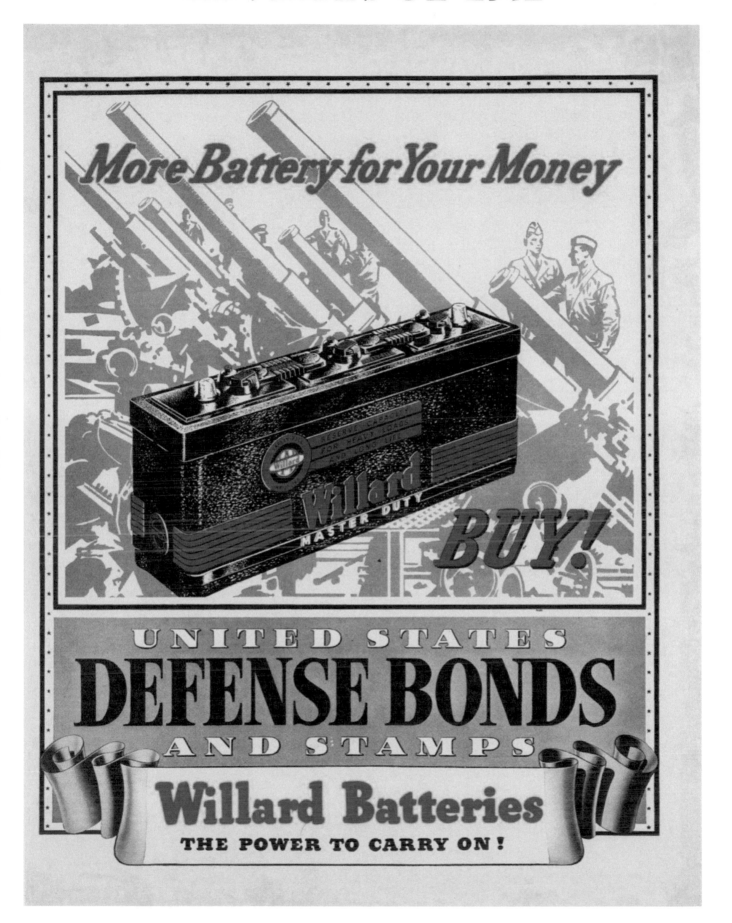

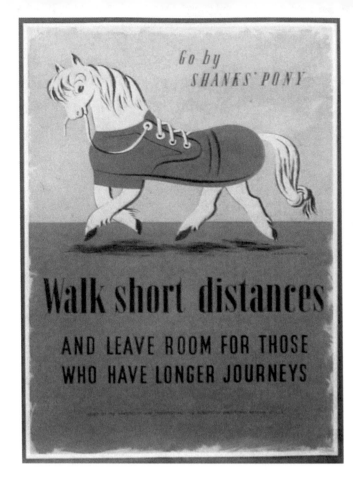

Volume 198
PRICE ONE SHILLING AND THREEPENCE

"TripleX" — the safety glass

The Illustrated London News.
1941

THE ILLUSTRATED LONDON NEWS.

THE WAR COMPLETELY AND EXCLUSIVELY ILLUSTRATED.

PRICE 1s. 3d.: BY INLAND POST, 1s. 5d.
Canada and Newfoundland, 23d. Foreign, 2s.

REGISTERED AS A NEWSPAPER FOR TRANSMISSION IN THE UNITED KINGDOM.
For conditions of sale and supply of "The Illustrated London News" set forth in another page.

PUBLISHING OFFICE : COMMONWEALTH HOUSE,
1, NEW OXFORD STREET LONDON, W.C.1

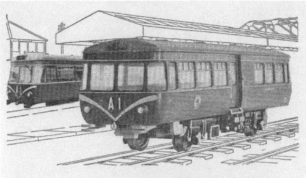

The Gift of being well-groomed

BRYLCREEM

THE PERFECT HAIR DRESSING

TONIGHT they're dining at the Mayfair; then on to a theatre and dancing till the early hours. Tomorrow they're full up too —not an evening before Friday week. You see them everywhere, the man-about-town and his constant companion—Brylcreem. However long the night, Brylcreem keeps his hair immaculate. Christmas is a busy time for them both, and he can always do with an extra jar. The big bottle with the pump attachment makes an ideal gift.

In bottles and tubes **1/**

Larger bottles **1/6 1/9 2/6**

Pumps to fit bottles . . . 2/-

At all Chemists and Hairdressers

Thanks to PENICILLIN
...He Will Come Home!

FROM ORDINARY MOLD—

the Greatest Healing Agent of this War!

On the gaudy, green-and-yellow mold above, called *Penicillium notatum* in the laboratory, grows the miraculous substance first discovered by Professor Alexander Fleming in 1928. Named penicillin by its discoverer, it is the most potent weapon ever developed against many of the deadliest infections known to man. Because research on molds was already a part of Schenley enterprise, Schenley Laboratories were well able to meet the problem of large-scale production of penicillin, when the great need for it arose.

When the thunderous battles of this war have subsided to pages of silent print in a history book, the greatest news event of World War II may well be the discovery and development — *not* of some vicious secret weapon that *destroys* — but of a weapon that *saves* lives. That weapon, of course, is penicillin.

Every day, penicillin is performing some unbelievable act of healing on some far battlefront. Thousands of men will return home who otherwise would not have had a chance. Better still, more and more of this precious drug is now available for civilian use ... to save the lives of patients of every age.

A year ago, production of penicillin was difficult, costly. Today, due to specially-devised methods of mass-production, in use by Schenley Laboratories, Inc. and the 20 other firms designated by the government to make penicillin, it is available in ever-increasing quantity, at progressively lower cost.

Listen to **"THE DOCTOR FIGHTS"** starring RAYMOND MASSEY. Tuesday evenings, C.B.S. See your paper for time and station.

SCHENLEY LABORATORIES, INC.
Lawrenceburg, Indiana

Producers of **PENICILLIN**-*Schenley*

COST OF LIVING 1941

A conversion of pre-decimal to decimal money

The Pound, 1971 became the year of decimalization when the pound became 100 new pennies. Prior to that the pound was equivalent to 20 shillings. Money prior to 1971 was written £/s/d. (d being for pence). Below is a chart explaining the monetary value of each coin before and after 1971.

Symbol	Before 1971	After 1971
£	Pound (240 pennies)	Pound (100 new pennies)
s	Shilling (12 pennies)	5 pence
d	Penny	¼ of a penny
¼d	Farthing	1 penny
½d	Halfpenny	½ pence
3d	Threepence	About 1/80 of a pound
4d	Groat (four pennies)	
6d	Sixpence (Tanner)	2½ new pence
2s	Florin (2 shillings)	10 pence
2s/6d	Half a crown (2 shillings and 6 pence)	12½ pence
5s	Crown	25 pence
10s	10 shilling note (10 bob)	50 pence
10s/6d	½ Guinea	52½ pence
21s	1 Guinea	105 pence

Prices are in equivalent to new pence today and on average throughout the UK.

Item	1941	Price equivalent today
Wages, average yearly	£195.00	£9,872.00
Average house price	£550.00	£27,775.00
Price of an average car	£310.00	£15,655.00
Litre of petrol	£0.02p	£1.20p
Flour 1.5kg	£0.03p	£1.36p
Bread (loaf)	£0.01p	£0.76p
Sugar 1kg	£0.04p	£1.87p
Milk 1 pint	£0.07p	£3.64p
Butter 250g	£0.04p	£2.22p
Cheese 400g	£0.05p	£2.40p
Potatoes 2.5kg	£0.03p	£1.53p
Bacon 400g	£0.12p	£5.86p
Beer (Pint)	£0.07p	£4.10p

How much did things cost in 1941?

Embassy cigarettes	10 for 9d (4p)
Wisdom toothbrushes	2/5 (12p) each
Eve toilet soap	3d (1½p) per bar
Palmolive toilet soap	4d (2p) per bar

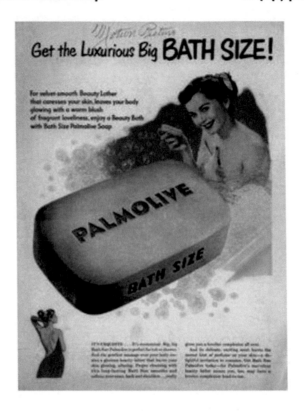

Vim	6d (2½p) per canister
Hartley's headlamp masks	10/6 (52½p) to 12/6 (62½p) each

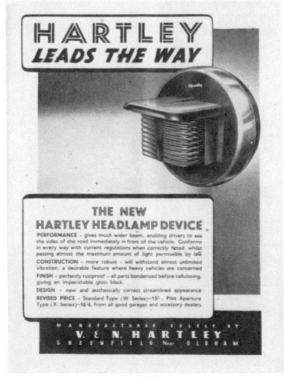

Gibbs Dentifrice   **7½d (3½p) and 1/3 (6½p) per tin**

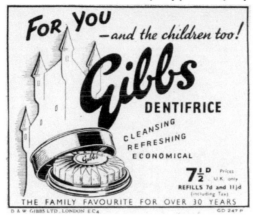

Cremola Pudding   **3d (1½p) and 6d (2½p) per pkt**

Rowntree's cocoa   **5d (2p) per ¼lb and 9½d (3½p) per ½lb**

Cadbury's Ration Chocolate   2½d (1p) per bar, the supply was very limited

Gamages advertised a shirt (with a spare collar)   6/11 (35p)

A pair of flannel trousers at 15/9 (78p)

A pair of shoes, all leather at 13/9 (68p)

And a mans lined raincoat for 1 guinea (that was £1/1/- (£1.05)).

BRITISH BIRTHS

Sir John Ernest Walker FRS FMedSci is a British chemist who won the Nobel Prize in Chemistry in 1997. He was born in Halifax, Yorkshire. As of 2015 Walker is Emeritus Director and Professor at the MRC Mitochondrial Biology Unit in Cambridge, and a Fellow of Sidney Sussex College, Cambridge. Walker was elected an EMBO Member in 1984. He shared his Nobel Prize with the American chemist Paul D. Boyer for their elucidation of the enzymatic mechanism underlying the synthesis of adenosine triphosphate. They also shared the prize with Danish chemist Jens C. Skou for research unrelated to theirs. Sir John was knighted in 1999 for services to molecular biology. He is a member of the Advisory Council for the Campaign for Science and Engineering. He was elected a Fellow of the Royal Society in 1995. Walker is also a Foreign Associate of the National Academy of Sciences and an Honorary Fellow of St Catherine's College, Oxford. He became a foreign member of the Royal Netherlands Academy of Arts and Sciences in 1999. In 2012 he was awarded the Copley Medal.

Graham Arthur Chapman was born on the 8th January 1941 and sadly passed away on the 4th October 1989. He was an English comedian, writer, actor, author, and one of the six members of the British surreal comedy group Monty Python. Graham Chapman and John Cleese began to write professionally for the BBC, initially for David Frost but also for Marty Feldman. Frost had recruited Cleese, and in turn Cleese decided he needed Chapman as a sounding board. Chapman also contributed sketches to the radio series I'm Sorry, I'll Read That Again and wrote material on his own and with Bill Oddie. In 1969, Chapman and Cleese joined the other Pythons, Michael Palin, Eric Idle, Terry Jones and Terry Gilliam, for their sketch comedy series Monty Python's Flying Circus. The group's writing was split into well-defined teams, with Chapman collaborating almost exclusively with John Cleese. In 1978, Chapman co-wrote the comedy film The Odd Job with McKenna, and starred as one of the main characters. Chapman wanted his friend Keith Moon to play a co-lead role alongside him, but Moon could not pass an acting test, so the part went to David Jason

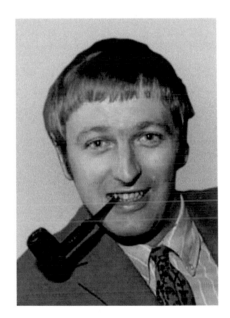

Michael David Apted was born on the 10th February 1941 and is an English director, producer, writer and actor. He began his career in television as a six-month trainee at Granada Television in Manchester, where he worked as a researcher. One of his first projects at Granada would become his best known: the Up series, which began in 1964 as a profile of 14 seven-year-old children for the current affairs series World In Action. During his seven-year stay at Granada, Apted also directed a number of episodes of Coronation Street, then written by Jack Rosenthal. Apted and Rosenthal went on to collaborate on a number of popular television and film projects including the pilot episodes for The Dustbin men and The Lovers. They worked together again in 1982 for the TV movie P'tang, Yang, Kipperbang, the first film commissioned by Britain's Channel 4. Michael Apted made his first feature film in 1972, The Triple Echo, starring Oliver Reed and Glenda Jackson, and he directed two films for David Puttnam.

Jeremy John Durham Ashdown, Baron Ashdown of Norton-sub-Hamdon, GCMG, CH, KBE, PC was born on the 27th February 1941 and passed away on the 22nd December 2018. He was also known as Paddy Ashdown. Paddy was a British politician and diplomat who served as Leader of the Liberal Democrats from 1988 to 1999. After his father's business collapsed, Ashdown passed the naval scholarship examination to pay for his school fees, but left before taking A-levels and joined the Royal Marines in 1959.

He served until 1972 and retired with the rank of captain. He served in Borneo during the Indonesia–Malaysia confrontation and the Persian Gulf, before training as a Swimmer Canoeist in 1965, after which he joined the elite Special Boat Section (now named the Special Boat Service) and commanded a Section in the Far East. He then went to Hong Kong in 1967 to undertake a full-time interpreter's course in Chinese, and returned to the UK in 1970 when he was given command of a Royal Marine company in Belfast.

David Cyril Eric Swarbrick was born on the 5th April 1941 and died on the 3rd June 2016. He was an English folk musician and singer-songwriter. He has been described by Ashley Hutchings as "the most influential fiddle player bar none" and his style has been copied or developed by almost every British and many world folk violin players who have followed him. He was one of the most highly regarded musicians produced by the second British folk revival, contributing to some of the most important groups and projects of the 1960s, and he became a much sought-after session musician, which led him throughout his career to work with many of the major figures in folk and folk rock music. A member of Fairport Convention from 1969, he is credited with assisting them to produce their seminal album Liege & Lief which initiated the British folk rock movement. This, and his subsequent career, helped create greater interest in British traditional music and were highly influential within mainstream rock. After 1970 he emerged as Fairport Convention's leading figure and guided the band through a series of important albums.

Gordon Fitzgerald Kaye was born on the 7th April 1941 and passed away on the 23rd January 2017 and was an English actor and singer. He made his TV debut as a railway guard in the BBC's Yorkshire mill drama Champion House in 1968. He appeared in the 1978 comedy short The Waterloo Bridge Handicap, starring Leonard Rossiter, and featured as Dines in the feature film version of Porridge alongside Ronnie Barker. He also appeared in the drama series All Creatures Great and Small and in the private detective series Shoestring. In 1982, David Croft sent Kaye the script for the pilot episode of 'Allo 'Allo! inviting him to play the central character of René Artois. He accepted and appeared in all 84 episodes (the main series ran from 1984, two years after the pilot, until 1992) and 1,200 performances of the stage version. Kaye died in a care home on the 23rd January 2017, at the age of 75 in Knaresborough. His funeral was held at Huddersfield Parish Church on 17 February 2017. His co-stars from 'Allo 'Allo! Vicki Michelle, Sue Hodge, and Kim Hartman attended, as did Ken Morley from Coronation Street, who gave a tribute.

Robert Frederick Chelsea Moore OBE and born on the 12th April 1941 and passed away on the 24th February 1993. He was an English professional footballer. He most notably played for West Ham United, captaining the club for more than ten years, and was the captain of the England national team that won the 1966 FIFA World Cup. He is widely regarded as one of the greatest defenders of all time, and was cited by Pelé as the greatest defender that he had ever played against. He won a total of 108 caps for his country, which at the time of his international retirement in 1973 was a national record. Moore's first brush with cancer was in 1964, two years before the historic World Cup win. He was diagnosed with testicular cancer, which he survived by having one testicle surgically removed. On the 14th February 1993, he publicly announced he was suffering from bowel and liver cancer; by this stage the cancer had spread. Three days later, he commentated on an England match against San Marino at Wembley, alongside his friend Jonathan Pearce. That was to be his final public appearance; seven days later on the 24th February, at 6:36 am, he died at the age of 51.

Julie Frances Christie was born on the 14th April 1940 and is a British actress and an icon of the "swinging London" era of the 1960s. Christie's breakthrough film role was in Billy Liar (1963). She came to international attention for her performances in Darling (1965), for which she won the Academy Award for Best Actress, and Doctor Zhivago (also 1965), the eighth highest-grossing film of all time after adjustment for inflation. In the following years, she starred in Fahrenheit 451 (1966), Far from the Madding Crowd (1967), Petulia (1968), The Go-Between (1971), McCabe & Mrs. Miller (1971), for which she received her second Oscar nomination, Don't Look Now (1973), Shampoo (1975), and Heaven Can Wait (1978).

She has received such accolades as an Academy Award, a Golden Globe Award, a BAFTA Award, and a Screen Actors Guild Award. She has appeared in six films that were ranked in the British Film Institute's 100 greatest British films of the 20th century, and in 1997, she received the BAFTA Fellowship.

Edward Stewart Mainwaring born on the 23rd April 1941 and passed away on the 9th January 2016. He was known as Ed "Stewpot" Stewart and was an English broadcaster. He attended Eagle House School, Sandhurst, Berkshire and St Edward's School, Oxford, and his broadcasting career began in Hong Kong. While touring there as bass player with a jazz group, he gained a job on a local radio station as a sports commentator, then as an announcer and, finally, as a disc jockey. He remained at this station for four years. In July 1965 Stewart became a DJ on the offshore radio station Radio London (Big L) where he became a household name before the marine offences bill was passed, and was its chief DJ by the time it closed on 14 August 1967. Ed Stewart became a regular presenter of the BBC television programme Top of the Pops in 1971. He also presented the children's programme Crackerjack from 1973 to 1979. Stewart died at the age of 74 on the 9th January 2016 in hospital in Bournemouth following a stroke.

Chris Curtis born Christopher Crummey was born on the 26th August 1941 and died on the 28th February 2005. He was an English drummer and singer with the 1960s beat band The Searchers. Curtis was an essential part of the Searchers' sound and contributed to the band's characteristic vocal harmonies with his distinctive voice, blending particularly well with the high-pitched voice of early band-mate Tony Jackson. Perhaps the finest example of this can be found in their rendition of "Ain't That Just Like Me", where Curtis sings the lead vocal, and Jackson chimes in with the recurring chorus. Curtis left The Searchers in 1966 after an extensive tour of the Philippines, Hong Kong and Australia, with the Rolling Stones. Accounts of the break-up differ but there were some significant incidents during the tour and Curtis had become unreliable. Curtis hated Australia and he was abusing a variety of substances to the point where he fell off the stage at one venue.

He died at home on 28 February 2005 at the age of 63.

Frederick Walter Stephen West was born on the 29th September 1941 and died on the 1st January 1995. He was an English serial killer who committed at least 12 murders between 1967 and 1987 in Gloucestershire. All the victims were young women. At least eight of these murders involved the Wests' sexual gratification and included rape, bondage, torture and mutilation; the victims' dismembered bodies were typically buried in the cellar or garden of the Wests' Cromwell Street home in Gloucester, which became known as the "House of Horrors". Fred is known to have committed at least two murders on his own, while Rose is known to have murdered Fred's stepdaughter, Charmaine. The couple were apprehended and charged in 1994.

Fred West fatally asphyxiated himself while on remand at HM Prison Birmingham on the 1st January 1995, at which time he and Rose were jointly charged with nine murders, and he with three further murders. In November 1995, Rose was convicted of ten murders and sentenced to ten life terms with a whole life order.

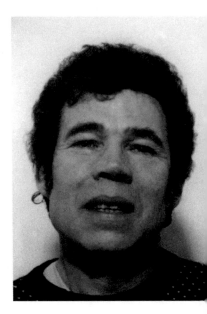

Jacqueline Jill Collins OBE was born on the 4th October 1937 and passed away on the 19th September 2015 and was an English romance novelist. Jackie Collins was born in 1937, in Hampstead, London, the younger daughter of Elsa Collins and Joseph William Collins, a theatrical agent whose clients later included Shirley Bassey, the Beatles, and Tom Jones. She began appearing in acting roles in a series of British B movies in the 1950s. Her parents then sent her to Los Angeles to live with her older sister, Joan, a Hollywood actress. She made a switch from acting onscreen to writing novels, and her first book, The World Is Full of Married Men (1968), became a best-seller. Four decades later she admitted she was a "school dropout" and "juvenile delinquent" when she was 15: "I'm glad I got all of that out of my system at an early age," she said, adding that she "never pretended to be a literary writer." Collins died on 19 September 2015, of breast cancer, two weeks before her 78th birthday. She had been diagnosed with stage 4 breast cancer more than six years before her death but kept her illness almost entirely to herself.

Patricia Stephanie Cole OBE was born on the 5th October 1941 and is an English stage, television, radio and film actress and was born in Solihull, Warwickshire, England. One of Cole's most recognised and popular roles was of Dr Beatrice Mason in the 1980s television series Tenko, a drama which chronicled the lives of British women in Singapore after the Japanese invasion and their consequent confinement in a Japanese prisoner of war camp. During this same period, Cole also played the elderly, paranoid and morose customer Mrs Delphine Featherstone, nicknamed "The Black Widow", in the BBC comedy Open All Hours. From 2004 to 2009, Cole appeared with Martin Clunes and Caroline Catz in the ITV comedy-drama, Doc Martin as Joan Norton, aunt of Clunes's character Dr Martin Ellingham. In April 2011, Cole joined the cast of Coronation Street, playing Sylvia Goodwin, the mother of regular character Roy Cropper. In August 2012. On Halloween 2018, Stephanie guest starred in the live episode of Inside No 9 entitled 'Dead Line', she played the role of Moira O'Keefe.

Hank Brian Marvin born Brian Robson Rankin, was born on the 28th October 1941 and is an English multi-instrumentalist, vocalist and songwriter and was born in Newcastle upon Tyne, Tyne and Wear, England. Sixteen-year-old Marvin and his Rutherford Grammar School friend, Bruce Welch, met Johnny Foster, Cliff Richard's manager, at The 2i's Coffee Bar in Soho, London. Foster was looking for a guitarist for Cliff Richard's UK tour and was considering Tony Sheridan. Instead he offered Marvin the position. Marvin joined the Drifters, as Cliff Richard's group was then known, provided there was a place for Welch. His first critically lauded, self-titled solo album of instrumentals, which featured guitar set to orchestrated backing, was released in 1969, following the first disbanding of the Shadows, in late 1968. In 1970, Marvin and Welch formed Marvin, Welch & Farrar, a vocal-harmony trio which failed to appeal to Shadows fans or to contemporary music fans. They became 'Marvin & Farrar' for a vocal album in 1973 and then reverted to the Shadows in late 1973.

Bruce Welch OBE was born on the 2nd November 1941 as Bruce Cripps and is an English guitarist, songwriter, producer, singer and businessman and grew up in Bognor Regis, Sussex, England. On moving to London, Bruce and Hank Marvin briefly operated as the Geordie Boys before enlisting in an outfit called the Drifters. In September 1958 Welch and Marvin joined the Drifters, later to become the Shadows, as Cliff Richard's backing band. As well as success with the Shadows, Welch acted as producer for (among others) Richard and songwriter for his ex-fiancée, Olivia Newton-John. Welch wrote several number 1 hit singles for Richard and for the Shadows. Among tunes or songs written or co-written by Welch are the Shadows' hits "Foot Tapper", "Theme for Young Lovers", and "The Rise and Fall of Flingel Bunt". After the Shadows disbanded in 1990, with Marvin deciding to tour with his own band, Welch's plans for his own tours did not fully materialise until 1998, when he formed Bruce Welch's Shadows. The group featured former Shadows bassist Alan Jones and keyboardist Cliff Hall, with Bob Watkins on drums. Phil Kelly and Barry Gibson shared lead guitar duties until Gibson's departure in 2000.

David Edward Leslie Hemmings was born on the 18th November 1941 and passed away on the 3rd December 2003. He was an English actor, director, and producer of film, television, and theatre. He co-founded the Hemdale Film Corporation in 1967. Hemmings became a star when cast in the lead of Blowup (1966). It was directed by Michelangelo Antonioni, who detested the "Method" way of acting. He sought to find a fresh young face for the lead in the film. The resulting film was a critical and commercial sensation for MGM which financed it, helping turn Hemmings and co-star Vanessa Redgrave into stars. Hemmings relocated to Hollywood. He played supporting roles in Man, Woman and Child (1983) and Airwolf (1984). He also worked extensively as a director on television programmes including the action-adventure drama series Quantum Leap the crime series Magnum, P.I. and two action-adventure series The A-Team and Airwolf. Hemmings died at age 62 of a heart attack, in Bucharest, Romania, on the film set of Blessed.

Prince William of Gloucester, William Henry Andrew Frederick was born on the 18th December 1941 and died on the 28th August 1972. He was a grandson of King George V and paternal cousin of Elizabeth II. At the time of his birth he was the fourth in line to the throne. A Cambridge and Stanford graduate, he joined the Foreign and Commonwealth Office, serving in Lagos and Tokyo, before returning to take over royal duties. He led an active life, flying Piper aircraft, trekking through the Sahara, and even ballooning. In 1947, Prince William was a page boy for his cousin Princess Elizabeth at her wedding to Philip, Duke of Edinburgh. The other page boy was Prince Michael of Kent. In 1953, he attended the coronation of Elizabeth II. A licensed pilot and President of the British Light Aviation Centre. In August 1972, he was competing in the Goodyear International Air Trophy near Wolverhampton. Shortly after their take-off and at a very low altitude, the Piper Cherokee banked abruptly to port, with an extreme increase in the rate of turn and corresponding loss of altitude; the wing hit a tree and sheared off, and the out-of-control plane flipped over and Prince William was killed.

Sir Alexander Chapman Ferguson CBE born on the 31st December 1941 was a former Scottish football manager and player and managed Manchester United from 1986 to 2013. Alex Ferguson played as a forward for several Scottish clubs, including Dunfermline Athletic and Rangers. While playing for Dunfermline, he was the top goalscorer in the Scottish league in the 1965–66 season. Towards the end of his playing career he also worked as a coach, then started his managerial career with East Stirlingshire and St Mirren. Ferguson then enjoyed a highly successful period as manager of Aberdeen, winning three Scottish league championships, four Scottish Cups and the UEFA Cup Winners' Cup in 1983. He briefly managed Scotland following the death of Jock Stein, taking the team to the 1986 World Cup. Alex Ferguson was appointed manager of Manchester United in November 1986. During his 26 years with Manchester United he won 38 trophies, including 13 Premier League titles, five FA Cups, and two UEFA Champions League titles. He was knighted in the 1999 Queen's Birthday Honours list for his services to the game.

Due to World War II sporting events were hit hard in the United Kingdom

1941 County Cricket Season

All first-class cricket was cancelled in the 1940 to 1944 English cricket seasons because of the Second World War; no first-class matches were played in England after Friday, 1st September 1939 until Saturday, 19th May 1945.

Ten matches were cancelled at the end of the 1939 English cricket season due to the German invasion of Poland on 1st September and the British government's declaration of war against Germany on Sunday 3rd September.

Although eleven first-class matches were arranged during the 1945 season following the final defeat of Germany in early May, it was not until the 1946 season that normal fixtures, including the County Championship and Minor Counties Championship, could resume. In contrast with much of the First World War, it was realised in the 1940s that cricket had its part to play in terms of raising both public morale and funds for charity. Efforts were made to stage matches whenever opportunity arose, especially if a suitable number of top players could be assembled. From the summer of 1941 onwards, teams such as the British Empire Eleven toured the country raising money for war charities.

At league cricket level, playing one-day matches, many competitions continued throughout the war: e.g., the Birmingham League, the Bradford League and the Lancashire League.

One venue where it would not be possible was The Oval, which was commandeered in 1939 and quickly turned into a prisoner of war camp, except that no prisoners were ever interned there. The playing area became a maze of concrete posts and wire fences.

Lord's was also due for requisition but it was spared and MCC was able to stage many public schools and representative games throughout the war. A highlight in 1940 was the one-day game in which Sir PF Warner's XI, including Len Hutton and Denis Compton (who top-scored with 73), beat a West Indies XI which included Learie Constantine and Leslie Compton (an honorary West Indian for the day).

Of the more regular wartime teams, the most famous were the British Empire XI and the London Counties XI which were established in 1940. Both played one-day charity matches, mostly in the south-east and often at Lord's. The British Empire XI was founded by Pelham Warner but featured mainly English county players. The politician Desmond Donnelly, then in the Royal Air Force, began the London Counties XI. In one match between the two, Frank Woolley came out of retirement and played against the new star batsman Denis Compton. The British Empire XI played between 34 and 45 matches per season from 1940 to 1944; the London Counties XI was credited with 191 matches from 1940 to 1945.

Although the teams were successful in raising money for charity, their main purpose was to help sustain morale. Many of the services and civil defence organisations had their own teams, some of them national and featuring first-class players.

County clubs encouraged their players to join the services but at the same time pleaded with their members to continue subscriptions "as an investment for the future". While some counties (notably Somerset and Hampshire) closed for the duration, others did arrange matches. Nottinghamshire played six matches at Trent Bridge in 1940 and Lancashire mooted a scheme for a regionalised county competition to include the minor counties, but it was not taken further.

The Masters 1941

The 1941 Masters Tournament was the eighth Masters Tournament, held April 3–6 at Augusta National Golf Club in Augusta, Georgia. Craig Wood won his first major title, three strokes ahead of runner-up Byron Nelson.

Wood opened with a 66 and led by five strokes after the first round. During the final round, Nelson caught him on the front nine and the two were briefly co-leaders. Wood scored a 34 (–2) over the final nine holes to secure the victory. The purse was $5,000 and the winner's share was $1,500

Player	Country	Year(s) won	R1	R2	R3	R4	Total	To par	Finish
Byron Nelson	United States	1937	71	69	73	70	283	–5	2
Jimmy Demaret	United States	1940	77	69	71	75	292	+4	T12
Ralph Guldahl	United States	1939	76	71	75	71	293	+5	T14
Gene Sarazen	United States	1935	76	72	74	75	297	+9	T19
Horton Smith	United States	1934, 1936	74	72	77	74	297	+9	T19

- The Masters did not have a 36-hole cut until 1957

Augusta National Golf Club, sometimes referred to as Augusta or the National, is one of the most famous and exclusive golf clubs in the world, located in Augusta, Georgia, United States. Unlike most private clubs which operate as non-profits, Augusta National is a for-profit corporation, and it does not disclose its income, holdings, membership list, or ticket sales.

Founded by Bobby Jones and Clifford Roberts, the course was designed by Jones and Alister Mackenzie and opened for play in 1932. Since 1934, the club has played host to the annual Masters Tournament, one of the four major championships in professional golf, and the only major played each year at the same course. It was the top ranked course in Golf Digest's 2009 list of America's 100 greatest courses and was the number ten-ranked course based on course architecture on Golf week Magazine's 2011 list of best classic courses in the United States.

Cheltenham Gold Cup 1941

Poet Prince was a British Thoroughbred racehorse who won the 1941 Cheltenham Gold Cup. He had earlier won the Stanley Chase at Aintree and went on to contest two more Gold Cups. He was unplaced when well-fancied in 1942 and finished fourth in 1945 at the age of thirteen. On 20 March 1941, Poet Prince was one of ten horses to contest the sixteenth running of the Cheltenham Gold Cup. David Sherbrooke had intended to ride the horse himself but was injured in a fall on the previous day and the ride went to Roger Burford. The 1940 winner Roman Hackle favourite ahead of Savon with Poet Prince third choice in the betting at odds of 7/2 whilst the other fancied runners included Red Rower (also trained by Ivor Anthony) and The Professor. In the race Poet Prince tracked Red Rower before taking the lead at the final obstacle. He drew away on the run-in and won by three lengths from Savon, with Red Rower a short head away in third place.

Triple Crown

2,000 Guineas

Lambert Simnel was a British Thoroughbred racehorse and sire, who raced during World War II and was best known for winning the classic 2000 Guineas in 1941. As a two-year-old he won once and finished second in the Dewhurst Stakes In the following spring he won the 2000 Guineas, beating a field which included the subsequent classic winners Owen Tudor and Sun Castle. He was beaten when favourite for the Derby and finished unplaced in the St Leger. He won once as a four-year-old in 1942 before being retired to stud. He stood as a breeding stallion in England and Argentina with limited success before his death in 1952.

St Leger

Sun Castle was a British Thoroughbred racehorse who raced during World War II and was best known for winning the classic St Leger in 1941. After showing promise as a two-year-old he finished third in the 2000 Guineas the following spring but ran poorly when strongly-fancied for the New Derby. He won a race at Newbury in August before taking the substitute New St Leger at Manchester Racecourse. He died in the following spring after contacting tetanus.

The Derby

Owen Tudor was a British Thoroughbred racehorse and sire. In a career that lasted from 1940 to 1942 he ran twelve times and won six races. His most important win came as a three-year-old in the summer of 1941 when he won the "New Derby" at Newmarket. During the Second World War many British racecourses were closed either for safety reasons or because the land was needed for military use. Epsom Downs Racecourse was used throughout the war for an anti-aircraft battery, leading to the creation of a substitute or "New" version of the race. Owen Tudor went on to win a substitute "Ascot Gold Cup" at Newmarket in 1942. At the end of that season he was retired to stud where he had considerable success as a sire of winners.

Evil Under the Sun is a work of detective fiction by British writer Agatha Christie, first published in the UK by the Collins Crime Club in June 1941 and in the US by Dodd, Mead and Company in October of the same year. The UK edition retailed at seven shillings and sixpence (7/6).

Hercule Poirot takes a quiet holiday at a secluded hotel in Devon. He finds that the other hotel guests include: Arlena Marshall, her husband Kenneth, and her step-daughter Linda; Horace Blatt; Major Barry, a retired officer; Rosamund Darnley, a former sweetheart of Kenneth; Patrick Redfern, and his wife Christine, a former teacher; Carrie Gardener, and her husband Odell; Reverend Stephen Lane; and Miss Emily Brewster, an athletic spinster.

During the initial part of his stay, Poirot notes that Arlena is a flirtatious woman, who flirts with Patrick much to the fury of his wife, and that her step-daughter hates her. One morning, Arlena heads out for a secret rendezvous at Pixy Cove. By midday, she is found dead by Patrick and Brewster while they are rowing. An examination by the local police surgeon reveals she had been strangled by a man.

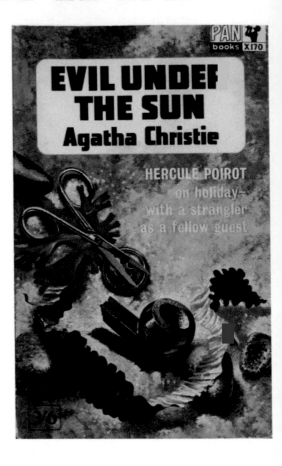

The Dry Salvages is the third poem of T. S. Eliot's Four Quartets, marking the beginning of the point when the series was consciously being shaped as a set of four poems. It was written and published in 1941 during the air-raids on Great Britain, an event that threatened him while giving lectures in the area. The poem is described as a poem of water and hope. It begins with images of the sea, water, and of Eliot's past; this water later becomes a metaphor for life and how humans act. These transitions into an image of a ringing bell and a discussion on time and prayer. Images of men drowning dominate the section before leading into how science and ideas on evolution separate mankind from properly understanding the past. This ends with Krishna stating that the divine will, and not future benefits or rewards, matters. The fourth section is a prayer to the Virgin Mary for fishermen, sailors, and the drowned. The end of The Dry Salvages starts with a discussion about how people attempt to see the future through various superstitious means. Then the narrator tries to convince the reader that resignation about death is necessary. However, such resignation should be viewed as pushing the self towards redemption and the eternal life in the next world. By acting properly, one would be able to overcome life and move towards the next world.

Hangover Square. Set against the backdrop of the days preceding Britain declaring war on Germany, the main character is George Harvey Bone, a lonely borderline alcoholic who has a form of dissociative identity disorder, referred to in the text as a "dead mood". An alternative diagnosis is temporal lobe epilepsy. He is obsessed with gaining the affections of Netta, a failed actress and one of George's circles of acquaintances with whom he drinks. Netta is repelled by George but, being greedy and manipulative, she and a mutual acquaintance, Peter, shamelessly exploit George's advances to extract money and drink from him.

During his disordered episodes, he is convinced he must kill Netta for the way she treats him. Upon recovering from these interludes, he cannot remember them. However outside these he embarks on several adventures, trying in vain to win Netta's affections, including a would-be romantic trip to Brighton which goes horribly wrong: Netta brings Peter along, and also a previously unknown man with whom she has sex in the hotel room next to George's.

Random Harvest is a novel written by James Hilton, first published in 1941. Like previous Hilton works, including Lost Horizon and Goodbye, Mr. Chips, the novel was immensely popular, placing second on The New York Times list of best-selling novels for the year.

It is set in the period immediately preceding the outbreak of the Second World War. It is told in the first person by Harrison, and by means of two extended external analepses tells the story of Charles Rainier, a wealthy businessman and politician, from the time he was invalided out of the army during World War I, his subsequent memory loss and partial recovery, his assuming control of the family business to his attempts to recover his memory just as Hitler invades Poland. The book is prefaced with this quote: German Official Report: "According to a British Official report, bombs fell at Random"'. The novel starts in 1937, and is narrated by Charles Rainier's secretary, Mr. Harrison. Charles and Mrs. Rainier ("Helen" in the novel) reside at Stourton, their country manor west of London, where she is the perfect hostess, and a young man named Woburn has been hired to catalogue the family library. One night Rainier recounts his story to Harrison, from the time he woke up in Liverpool in 1919, having lost two years of his life.

The Oxford Dictionary of Quotations, first published by the Oxford University Press in 1941, is an 1100-page book listing short quotations that are common in English language and culture. The book begins with a preface explaining the term "quotation". The dictionary has been compiled from extensive evidence of the quotations that are actually used in the way they have been listed. This book is not—like many quotations dictionaries—a subjective anthology of the editor's favourite quotations, but an objective selection of the quotations which are most widely known and used. Popularity and familiarity are the main criteria for inclusion, although no reader is likely to be familiar with all the quotations in this dictionary. The quotations are drawn from novels, plays, poems, essays, speeches, films radio and television broadcasts, songs, advertisements, and even book titles. It is difficult to draw the line between quotations and similar sayings like proverbs, catch-phrases, and idioms. These are usually included if they can be traced to a particular originator. Catch-phrases are included if there is evidence that they are widely remembered or used. Quotations are also cross-referenced. For example, on looking up Napoleon's quotation about Britain being a nation of shopkeepers, one also finds Adam Smith, who said it first.

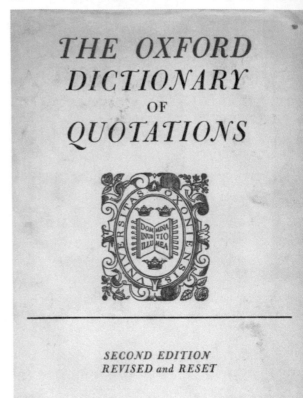

Black Lamb and Grey Falcon: A Journey Through Yugoslavia is a travel book written by Dame Rebecca West, published in 1941 in two volumes by Macmillan in the UK and by The Viking Press in the US.

The book is over 1,100 pages in modern editions and gives an account of Balkan history and ethnography during West's six-week trip to Yugoslavia in 1937. West's objective was "to show the past side by side with the present it created".

Publication of the book coincided with the Nazi Invasion of Yugoslavia, and West added a foreword highly praising the Yugoslavs for their brave defiance of Germany. The book's epigraph reads: "To my friends in Yugoslavia, who are now all dead or enslaved".

The character of "Constantine" is supposedly based on Stanislav Vinaver. Anica Savić Rebac, under the name of Milica, appears not only as a new friend, but also as the intellectual guide who eventually reveals to Rebecca West the rituals which would lead the author to the title metaphor of her vision of the Balkans.

Citizen Kane. After his death, the life of Charles Foster Kane - newspaper magnate and all-round larger-than-life American - is told from the perspective of those who knew him.

A newspaper reporter is interviewing those in Kane's life hoping to learn the meaning of Kane's last word, Rosebud. Kane was sent to a boarding school at a young age after his mother struck it rich thanks to a mining claim that was signed over to her in lieu of rent. He came into his vast fortune at the age of 25 and promptly bought a newspaper. His idea of news was to make it as much as report it and along with his good friend, Jedediah Leland, had a rollicking good time. Unsuccessful in his bid for political office, his relationships with those around him begin to deteriorate and he dies, old and alone, whispering the word Rosebud.

Budget:$839,727 (estimated)
Gross USA: $1,585,634
Cumulative Worldwide Gross: $1,594,107

Run time is 1h 59mins

Trivia

Despite all the publicity, the film was a box-office flop and was quickly consigned to the RKO vaults. At 1941's Academy Awards the film was booed every time one of its nine nominations was announced. It was only re-released to the public in the mid-'50s.

To keep studio execs off his back, Orson Welles claimed the cast and crew were "in rehearsal" during the first few days of shooting, when in fact they were actually shooting the film. It took a number of days before the studio caught on.

To keep studio execs off his back, Orson Welles claimed the cast and crew were "in rehearsal" during the first few days of shooting, when in fact they were actually shooting the film. It took a number of days before the studio caught on.

Goofs

At the end of her interview with the reporter Thompson, Susan Alexander Kane says, "Come around sometime and tell me the story of your life," but as she says this her mouth is not moving.

When Jim Gettys reveals Kane's mistress to his wife, Gettys shouts to Kane, "We've got proof! It will look bad in the papers" Looking closely, he actually said, "...It will look good in the papers..."

When Susan Alexander Kane is doing the jigsaw puzzle by the fireplace, in the first wide shot it's clear that the puzzle is almost complete, but in the subsequent close-up the puzzle has hardly been started.

Maltese Falcon. Spade and Archer is the name of a San Francisco detective agency. That's for Sam Spade and Miles Archer. The two men are partners, but Sam doesn't like Miles much. A knockout, which goes by the name of Miss Wonderly, walks into their office; and by that night everything's changed. Miles is dead. And so is a man named Floyd Thursby. It seems Miss Wonderly is surrounded by dangerous men.

There's Joel Cairo, who uses gardenia-scented calling cards. There's Kasper Gutman, with his enormous girth and feigned civility. Her only hope of protection comes from Sam, who is suspected by the police of one or the other murder. More murders are yet to come, and it will all be because of these dangerous men -- and their lust for a statuette of a bird: the Maltese Falcon.

Box Office
Budget: $375,000 (estimated)
Cumulative Worldwide Gross: $1,255,000

Run time 1h 40mins

Trivia

Three of the statuettes still exist and are conservatively valued at over $1 million each. This makes them some of the most valuable film props ever made; indeed, each is now worth more than three times what the film cost to make.

Two "Maltese Falcons" were used because Humphrey Bogart accidentally dropped the original during shooting. It is on display in the movie museum at Warner Bros. studios; its tail feathers are visibly dented from when Bogart dropped it.

Warner Bros. planned to change the name of the film to "The Gent from Frisco" because the novel's title had already been used for The Maltese Falcon (1931). The studio eventually agreed to keep the original title at John Huston's insistence.

Goofs

Spade doesn't wear rings or a watch throughout the movie except for one scene. At one point he walks into his office wearing a wedding band on his left hand, another large ring on his right hand and an expensive-looking wristwatch. He sits down to have a quick chat with his secretary where the rings and watch are in plain view. He then walks through a doorway into his inner office and the rings and watch are gone.

When Sam first goes to see Gutman in 12C, as he walks down the corridor we can see that directly in front of him is a chair, a table with flowers on and a silhouette of a diamond framed window and the flowers on the wall, but when he leaves we can see two chairs either side of the table and the diamond frame silhouette is not there.

Dumbo. Mrs. Jumbo sadly looks on how babies are delivered by stork to colleague circus-animals but as even a baby elephant makes a most cumbersome package, so her so is just last to arrive, but soon becomes a laughing stock for the jealous herd because of his more than jumbo-size ears, so he gets nick-named Dumbo. When she can't stomach the public making fun of her firstborn, she is locked up as mad elephant, and the taunted kid finds himself all alone; well, except for a self-appointed mentor-protector, Timothy Q. Mouse -subsize, yet ideal to scare the jealous herd- who keeps motivating Dumbo. Alas inspiring the circus director to make Dumbo the top (literally) of an elephant pyramid stunt literally brings the house down, so he's demoted to clown. When everything seems lost, they accidentally discover how they ended up in a tree with a bunch of crows...

Box Office
Budget:$950,000 (estimated)
Cumulative Worldwide Gross: $3,731,000

Run time 1h 4mins.

Trivia

Initially Walt Disney was uninterested in making this movie. To get him interested, story men Joe Grant and Dick Huemer wrote up the film as instalments which they left on Walt's desk every morning. Finally, he ran into the story department saying, "This is great! What happens next?"

Cels for this film are the rarest in the industry. The animators, after the scene was safely "in the can," would spread the used cels in the corridors and go sliding on them. In addition, the grey paint (used for so many of the elephant skins) would "pop" when the cel was flexed. Many cels were destroyed this way.

In December 1941, Time Magazine planned to have Dumbo on the cover to commemorate its success, but it was dropped due to the Japanese attack on Pearl Harbour.

Goofs

In all the scenes with rain, lightning and thunder are shown to be going off at the same time. Light travels faster than sound, so in reality, there would first be a flash of lightning and then a clap of thunder.

The footbridge of the elephants' wagon changes look from scene to scene. When the elephants enter during the train loading, the bridge has wooden pads to back it. The pads disappear while the bridge is used to free Matriarch. The footbridge has a sudden change of color after Matriarch took the big toss. There is another change of color after the upper part of the wagon falls down on Matriarch's head to finish the incident.

When Timothy tells Dumbo to blow a "great big one," Dumbo's collar disappears when he does so. In the next shot, it's back.

The Wolf Man. "Even a man who is pure at heart/And says his prayers by night/May become a wolf when the wolf-bane blooms/And the moon is full and bright." Upon first hearing these words, Larry Talbot (Lon Chaney) dismisses them as childish federal.

After all, this is the 20th Century; how can a human being turn into a werewolf? Talbot soon learns how when he attempts to rescue Jenny Williams (Fay Helm) from a nocturnal attack by a wolf. Collapsing, Talbot discovers upon reviving that Jenny is dead-and, lying by her side, is not the body of a beast, but of a gypsy named Bela (Bela Lugosi). The son of fortune teller Maleva (Maria Ouspenskaya), Bela was a Lycanthrope, or "wolf man." And now that he has been bitten by Bela, Talbot is cursed to suffer the torments of the damned whenever the moon is full.

Box Office
Budget: $180,000 (estimated)

Run time 1h 10mins

Trivia
In Curt Siodmak's original script for the film, whether or not Lawrence Talbot really underwent a physical transformation to a werewolf or if the transformation simply occurred in his mind was left ambiguous. The Wolf Man was never to appear onscreen. Ultimately, the studio determined that Talbot's literal transformation into a werewolf would be more appealing to the audience and thus more profitable. The script was revised accordingly.

The Wolfman battled a bear in one scene but unfortunately the bear ran away during filming. What few scenes were filmed was put into the theatrical trailer.

This film marks the first of five appearances by Lon Chaney Jr. as the Wolf Man for Universal Studios. Out of Universal's classic canon of monsters, Chaney was the only actor to portray the same character in each of the studio's classic films and sequels.

Goofs
Bela the Gypsy transforms into an actual wolf, not a wolf/man. When his body is discovered, his feet are bare but he is wearing a shirt and trousers. The wolf killed by Larry Talbot was not wearing any clothing.

When the gypsy woman, Maleva, reaches out with one hand to lift the lid of Bela's casket, it is obviously not being lifted by her fingertips, but by an unseen crewman on the off-camera end of the lid.

After Larry Talbot has been bitten, we see the Talbot family butler open the living room door to let Larry stumble in, all in long shot. Then it cuts to a close up that repeats the action exactly, including the butler reopening the door.

Suspicion. While travelling to the countryside of England by train, the repressed and shy Lina McLaidlaw meets the reckless playboy Johnnie Aysgarth crashing her first class cabin with a third class ticket. When they meet each other again, Johnnie overhears a conversation of her father about her heritage and courts Lina who immediately falls in love for him. They get married and when they return from their fancy honeymoon, Lina discovers that Johnnie is a broken gambler that borrows money from his friends to live in a high standard. Then she finds out that he is also a liar, and after receiving his old friend and partner in a real estate business, Beaky, in their home, Lina believes that Johnnie intends to kill Beaky. However, they decide to travel to Paris to dissolve their partnership. When two detectives come to their house to investigate the mysterious death of Beaky in Paris, Lina believes Johnnie is the murderer, and she will be his next victim.

Box Office
Budget:$1,103,000 (estimated)

Run time 1h 39mins

Trivia

In interviews, Sir Alfred Hitchcock said that an RKO executive ordered that all scenes in which Cary Grant appeared menacing be excised from the movie. When the cutting was completed, the movie ran only fifty-five minutes. The scenes were later restored, Hitchcock said, because he shot each piece of film so that there was only one way to edit them together properly.

Joan Fontaine's performance in this movie is the only Oscar-winning performance that Sir Alfred Hitchcock directed.

Originally, this movie was intended as a B movie to star George Sanders and Anne Shirley. Then when Sir Alfred Hitchcock became involved, the budget increased, and Sir Laurence Olivier and Frances Dee were to star.

Goofs

According to the invitation shown on screen, the hunt ball is on March 7, but the telegram that persuades Lina to attend the ball is dated March 8.

In the dinner scene at her parent's house after Lina's walk with Johnnie, the glasses of water in front of her parents are both full, but during the course of their conversation with Lina, neither of them takes a drink of water. When Lina leaves to answer the phone, the glasses are empty.

Why the reference to "Richard Palmer", a murderer who killed a man in a drinking bet before "going on to kill a lot of other people", when the (very famous) real life murderer was William Palmer?

The Little Foxes. In 1900, in the Southern town of Linnet, the notorious Hubbard family is hated by the residents since they exploit the poor and the black people in their business. Regina Giddens, née Hubbard, is married with Horace Giddens, who is a good man that is interned in a hospital in Baltimore due to a heart condition. They are estranged and they have a daughter, the naive Alexandra Giddens that has a crush on the local David Hewitt but she is controlled by her merciless mother. Regina's brothers are the exploitative Ben Hubbard, who is single, and Oscar Hubbard, who is married with the wounded Birdie, and they have a son, the scum Leo that works in a bank. Oscar and Regina have made arrangements to marry Leo with Alexandra. When Ben and Oscar invite the wealthy businessman William Marshall to come to Linnet to build a mill to improve their business and pay low wages to the locals, they need US$ 75,000.00 from Regina. She manipulates Alexandra to bring Horace back home to convince him to lend the money. However, Horace does not accept the business and Leo steals his railroad bonds from the safe in the bank to invest in the business with Marshall, expecting to return the money without Horace noticing. Bur Horace goes to the bank and finds the embezzlement. What will Horace and Alexandra do?

Run time 1h 56mins

Trivia

William Wyler encouraged Bette Davis to see Tallulah Bankhead's Broadway performance. Davis was not keen on the idea but agreed to do so, regretting it instantly as she realized that she was now forced to play the character in a very different manner. Bankhead played her as a fighter; Davis' interpretation was of a cold, calculating and conniving woman.

Bette Davis was a contract player for Warner Brothers at the time, earning $3000 a week. When she heard how much Warner's was receiving for her services she demanded a share of the payment.

Shot during one of Los Angeles' hottest heatwaves in years, with temperatures on the soundstages frequently rising above 100 degrees.

Goofs

When Regina returns home to find Horace in her part of the house, she clearly takes her left glove off before walking towards the staircase. Seconds later, after Horace tells her about the investment in the cotton mill, she turns around at the bottom of the staircase and takes her left glove off again.

On the night before Alexandria leaves for Baltimore when she leans over the railing after Aunt Birdie is slapped: In the wide shot her right hand is about 20 inches from the column, then in the close-up her hand is just inches from the column.

When Zan is getting her hair washed it is much shorter than it is when it is dry and styled.

Sergeant York. After meeting Gracie Williams, the love of his life, the Tennessee backwoodsman and exceptional sharpshooter, Alvin C. York, decides to straighten out and settle down. With great effort, Alvin finally manages to come up with the large amount for a beautiful patch of land; however, when the seller breaks his promise, the wronged man seeks retribution, only to be stopped by a nearly fatal bolt of lightning. Unexpectedly, under the wing of the community's pastor, Rosier Pile, York finds solace in religion; nevertheless, when WWI breaks out, his application as a conscientious objector to avoid service will be rejected, complicating further his already thorny pacifist conflict. Sooner or later, York will have to come face-to-face with his greatest fear: to kill or be killed. Will York's extensive hunting knowledge help him outsmart the Germans and their devastating machine guns in the blood-soaked battlefields of the Meuse-Argonne Offensive on October 8, 1918?

Box Office
Budget: $1,400,000 (estimated)
Gross USA: $16,361,885

Run time 2h 14mins

Trivia

Gary Cooper's acceptance speech typified so many of the actor's performances when he said "It was Sergeant Alvin C. York who won this award; Shucks, I've been in this business sixteen years and sometimes dreamed I might get one of these things. That's all I can say! Funny, when I was dreaming, I always made a good speech." As he left the stage, he forgot the Oscar on the podium.

The highest grossing film of 1941. Adjusted for inflation, it still remains one of the highest grossing films of all time.

There were stories at the time of young men leaving the movie theater after seeing the film and signing up immediately after. (War fever was particularly high in the USA at the time as the attack on Pearl Harbour had just happened.)

Because of the 1941 draft, the filmmakers had difficulty finding enough young male actors to play the soldiers and were forced to hire students from local universities.

Goofs

After being struck by lightning, Alvin goes into the church. He was drenched by the heavy rainstorm, yet his clothes and hair are barely wet as he walks through the church.

A guide wire is visible that is connected to a tree stump where the stump is being removed by a horse. The guide wire is visible behind the stump as the stump pulls free from the ground.

The Lady Eve. After one year in Amazon researching snakes, the naive ophidiologist Charles Pike returns to the United States in a transatlantic. Charles is the son of the Connecticut's brewery millionaire Mr. Pike and disputed by gold diggers. The swindlers Jean Harrington (Barbara Stanwyck), her father "Colonel" Harrington and their friend Gerald plan a confidence trick on Charles, but unexpectedly Jean falls in love with Charles and she calls off the scheme. However Charles's bodyguard Muggsy discovers that Jean is a con-artist and the disappointed Charles leaves Jean. Sometime later, in New York, the trio of con-artists meets their friend "Sir" Alfred McGlennan Keith in the horse races and they learn that "Sir" Alfred belonged to the high-society of Connecticut based on the reputation he had built. Jean sees the opportunity to take revenge at Charles, and she travels to the house of her "aunt" pretending to be the British noble Lady Eve. Mr. Pike promotes a party for Lady Eve and she seduces Charles that proposes her. But her intention is to get even with Charles.

Box Office
Cumulative Worldwide Gross: $13,020

Run time 1h 34mins

Trivia

With so many people on the set, Preston Sturges dressed eccentrically so that he would stand out. He usually wore either a brightly coloured beret or a hat with a feather in it. This sartorial splendour led to his being dubbed the worst-dressed man in Hollywood.

Barbara Stanwyck and Henry Fonda rarely retired to their dressing rooms between takes. Instead, they hung out with Preston Sturges, listening to his stories and reviewing - and often re-writing - their lines.

Friends of Preston Sturges who read the script tried to convince him to cut the number of pratfalls taken by Henry Fonda, arguing that they were too much of a good thing. Sturges didn't agree, and the slapstick bits later proved to be among the film's highlights.

Goofs

When Charles and Jean are standing on the deck talking, the ambient, background sounds - of people talking and birds singing - can be heard running on a loop. The scene lasts several minutes, but the ambient sounds repeat every several seconds.

During the poker game on ship Eve asks Hopsy how much he's down and he says about $2000, She deals the next hand giving him 4 queens and the betting ensues. The pot grows to $4200 or a profit to the winner of $2100. After Hopsy wins, Eve asks again how far he's down and he answers about $1000, however he should be about $100 to the good.

When "Colonel" Harrington talks to Jean in her cabin the morning after Pike proposes, the shadow of a spotlight moves up and out of frame.

Meet John Doe. Mad with anger for having to compose one last article after being fired, the calculating columnist, Anne Mitchell, pens a flaming but utterly fictitious letter by the fictional author, "John Doe", who protests against the world's perpetual injustices. Threatening to commit suicide on Christmas Eve, John's desperate manifesto strikes a chord with an army of captivated readers all over America, and as a result, the newspaper decides to embody the ultimatum's spirit in the person of the down-at-the-heels vagabond and former pitcher, Long John Willoughby--the nation's next-door hero. Now, as Ann's creation and the unstoppable "John Doe Movement" take the country by surprise, artful manipulation, rampant corruption, and above all, corporate greed, threaten to put a premature end to the noble idea. Will the world ever find out the truth?

Academy Awards Nominee Oscar

Best Writing, Original Story: Richard Connell & Robert Presnell

Run time 2h 3mins

Trivia

Frank Capra didn't want anyone to play John Doe except Gary Cooper, who agreed to the part (without reading a script) for two reasons: he had enjoyed working with Capra on Mr. Deeds Goes to Town (1936) and he wanted to work with Barbara Stanwyck.

Four different endings were filmed, but all were ultimately deemed unsatisfactory during previews. A letter from an audience member suggested a fifth ending, which Frank Capra liked and used in the finished film.

This was the first and only commercial feature film produced by Frank Capra Productions. Frank Capra owned two-thirds of the company and Robert Riskin the remaining third.

Goofs

During the montage showing John Doe Clubs gaining in popularity, close-ups of a map are shown with flags being pinned up for every new club. At the end of the montage, the camera pulls back to show a map of the entire US. However, the final map has substantially fewer flags pinned to it than what was shown during the close-ups.

When Henry is telling John about Morton's plans for the John Doe clubs, he lights a match but holds it an inch above the cigarette that he supposed to light it with. At the end of the scene, Henry presses the end of the cigarette into a plate to extinguish it, but the cigarette at this point is no longer burning and the end is already bent over showing that it had already been pressed into the plate in an early take.

The collar of John Doe's coat is alternately up and down between shots when Ann is persuading him not to jump off the roof.

Adventures of Captain Marvel. On a scientific expedition to Siam young Billy Batson is given the ability to change himself into the super-powered Captain Marvel by the wizard Shazam, who tells him his powers will last only as long as the Golden Scorpion idol is threatened.

 Finding the idol, the scientists realize it could be the most powerful weapon in the world and remove the lenses that energize it, distributing them among themselves so that no one would be able to use the idol by himself. Back in the US, Billy Batson, as Captain Marvel, wages a battle against an evil, hooded figure, the Scorpion, who hopes to accumulate all five lenses, thereby gaining control of the super-powerful weapon.

Box Office
Budget:$138,588 (estimated)

Filmed in 12 episodes

Run time 2h 36mins

Trivia

CHAPTER TITLES: 1. Curse of the Scorpion; 2. The Guillotine; 3. Time Bomb; 4. Death Takes the Wheel; 5. The Scorpion Strikes; 6. Lens of Death; 7. Human Targets; 8. Boomerang; 9. Dead Man's Trap; 10.Doom Ship; 11.Valley of Death; 12.Captain Marvel's Secret.

This was the first depiction of a comic book superhero on film.

The effect of Captain Marvel flying was achieved by filming an oversized dummy that was slid along a fine wire.

The cast member under the Scorpion's hood, momentarily visible and identifiable when he is accidentally unmasked in one episode, is not the same actor who is eventually unmasked as the actual Scorpion in the final episode.

Goofs

While chasing Betty along the top of a dam, the bad guy is confronted by Captain Marvel; he fires seven shots out of his six shot revolver at him.

In chapter 10, Billy Batson, wearing a raincoat and life jacket over his suit, changes to Captain Marvel. When he changes back to Billy, the raincoat and life jacket are gone.

In Chapter 11 as Captain Marvel heaves a tree trunk from the road way, a crew member steps out from behind a large rock and, realizing his mistake, steps back out of sight.

Dr. Jekyll and Mr. Hyde. In London, in 1887, prominent physician Henry Jekyll incurs the ire of his older colleagues because of his experiments and views on the possibility of separating the good and evil aspects of man's nature.

Henry is deeply in love with Beatrix Emery, the daughter of Sir Charles Emery, who likes Henry, but is concerned over his radical ideas and open display of affection for Bea. Henry throws himself into his work and has enough success experimenting with rabbits and guinea pigs to make him confident that the serum he has developed will work for humans. Hoping to try the serum out on Sam Higgins, a man who went mad after being in a gas works explosion, Henry rushes to the hospital but discovers that Higgins has just died. Henry then decides to take the serum himself and is briefly transformed, in both thought and countenance, into an evil alter ego. After taking an antidote to turn himself back to normal, Henry tells his butler, Poole, that strange voice he heard was a "Mr. Hyde".

Run time 1h 53mins

Trivia

Spencer Tracy originally wanted a realistic approach, whereby Dr. Jekyll would commit violent deeds in a neighbourhood where he was unknown after drinking alcohol or taking drugs. He was disappointed that the producers, having bought the screenplay from Dr. Jekyll and Mr. Hyde (1931), insisted on virtually remaking the earlier film.

The film was a notorious critical failure when released, although it eventually made a profit of $2 million around the world. Spencer Tracy later said it was by far the least favourite of the films he had starred in, and that his performance was "awful". The New York Times famously described it as "not so much evil incarnate as ham rampant ... more ludicrous than dreadful."

When author W. Somerset Maugham visited the set during the filming, he supposedly watched a bit of Spencer Tracy's performance and asked sardonically, "Which one is he now, Jekyll or Hyde?"

Goofs

After attacking Ivy in her room Jekyll runs away from her house. As he approaches a carriage his hat flies off and he keeps running around a corner. In the next shot, from the other end of the corner, his hat is securely on his head.

In the scene where Hyde visits Ivy, he is sitting in a chair eating some grapes. In close-up he can be seen putting the last grape into his mouth with his right hand; but in the next medium shot, showing Hyde in the foreground and Ivy in the background, he is feeding himself with his left hand.

When Jekyll and Lanyon drop off Ivy at her home, a wire is visibly attached to Ivy. It evidently helps her as she falls out of the carriage, and again supports her weight as Jekyll "carries" her inside.

MUSIC 1941

Artist	Single	Reached number one	Weeks at number one
1941			
Artie Shaw and His Orchestra	Frenesi	21st December 1940	13
Glenn Miller and His Orchestra	Song of the Volga Boatmen	15th March 1941	1
Artie Shaw and His Orchestra	Frenesi	22nd March 1941	1
Jimmy Dorsey and His Orchestra	Amapola	29th March 1941	1
Jimmy Dorsey and His Orchestra	My Sister and I	7th June 1941	1
Jimmy Dorsey and His Orchestra	Maria Elena	14th June 1941	1
Swing and Sway with Sammy Kaye	Daddy	21st June 1941	1
Jimmy Dorsey and His Orchestra	My Sister and I	28th June 1941	1
Jimmy Dorsey and His Orchestra	Maria Elena	5th July 1941	1
Swing and Sway with Sammy Kaye	Daddy	12th July 1941	6
Jimmy Dorsey and His Orchestra	Green Eyes	30th August 1941	4
Jimmy Dorsey and His Orchestra	Blue Champagne	27th September 1941	1
Freddy Martin and His Orchestra	Piano Concerto in B Flat	4th October 1941	7
Glenn Miller and His Orchestra with Tex Beneke	Chattanooga Choo Choo	29th November 1941	3
Glenn Miller and His Orchestra with Ray Eberle	Elmer's Tune	20th December 1941	1
Glenn Miller and His Orchestra with Tex Beneke	Chattanooga Choo Choo	27th December 1941	2

Artie Shaw and His Orchestra

" Frenesi "

"**Frenesi**" is a musical piece originally composed by Alberto Domínguez for the marimba, and adapted as a jazz standard by Leonard Whitcup and others. The word frenesí is Spanish for "frenzy". A hit version recorded by Artie Shaw and His Orchestra (with an arrangement by William Grant Still) reached number one on the Billboard pop chart on the 21st December, 1940, staying for thirteen weeks and was inducted into the Grammy Hall of Fame in 1982.

The Artie Shaw recording was used in the soundtrack of the 1980 film Raging Bull.

The track regained number one spot on the 22nd March for one more week.

Glenn Miller and His Orchestra

"Song of the Volga Boatmen"

"**Song of the Volga Boatmen**" is a well-known traditional Russian song collected by Mily Balakirev, and published in his book of folk songs in 1866. It was sung by burlaks, or barge-haulers, on the Volga River. Balakirev published it with only one verse (the first). The other two verses were added at a later date. Ilya Repin's famous painting Barge Haulers on the Volga depicts such burlaks in Tsarist Russia toiling along the Volga.

The song was popularised by Feodor Chaliapin, and has been a favourite concert piece of bass singers ever since. Glenn Miller's jazz arrangement took the song to #1 in the charts in 1941. Russian composer Alexander Glazunov based one of the themes of his symphonic poem "Stenka Razin" on the song.

Jimmy Dorsey and His Orchestra with Bob Eberly

"Amapola"

"**Amapola**" is a 1920 song by Spanish American composer José María Lacalle García, who also wrote the original lyrics in Spanish.

A popular recorded version was made later by the Jimmy Dorsey Orchestra with vocalists Helen O'Connell and Bob Eberly; this was released by Decca Records as catalogue number 3629 and arrived on the Billboard charts on the 14th March, 1941, where it stayed for 14 weeks and reached #1 for one week. This version was remembered by American soldiers in World War II and sung with irony as they fought in France and saw the poppies of Flanders Fields. Another English-language version for the American market was recorded by Spike Jones and his City Slickers in the characteristic comic style of his band.

Jimmy Dorsey and His Orchestra with Bob Eberly

"My Sister and I"

"**My Sister and I**" is a song written by Hy Zaret, Joan Whitney and Alex Kramer, recorded by Jimmy Dorsey, with vocals by Bob Eberly. It hit number one on the Billboard charts on the 7th June 1941 and again on the 28th June for one week.

Sheet music of the time shows a boy and girl in Dutch clothing, with windmills in the background. Under the title appears the description, "As inspired by the Current Best Seller 'My Sister and I' by Dirk van der Heide." The lyric is in the voice of a child who has—with a sister—left a war zone by boat and begun a new life abroad. The line "the fear/That came from a troubled sky" along with the song's release date implies the evacuation of children from the countries ravaged by World War II, such as the London Blitz the previous winter.

Jimmy Dorsey and His Orchestra with Bob Eberly

"Maria Elena"

"María Elena" is a 1932 popular song written by Lorenzo Barcelata. It was published by Peer International Corporation of Mexico.

The song was a hit for the Jimmy Dorsey orchestra with Bob Eberly doing the vocals. The recording was made on the 19th March, 1941 by Decca Records as catalogue number 3698. The flip side was "Green Eyes." The record first reached the Billboard charts on the 16th May, 1941 and lasted 17 weeks on the chart, peaking at #1 on the 14th June, 1941 and again on the 5th July for another week. Since "Green Eyes" was also a #1 hit, this was a major double-sided hit recording. In the same year the Wayne King Orchestra also had a #2 hit with "Maria Elena".

Swing and Sway with Sammy Kaye

"Daddy"

"Daddy" is a song recorded by Sammy Kaye, using the band name "Swing and Sway with Sammy Kaye", with vocals by The Kaye Choir. It hit number one in the Billboard on the 21st June, 1941. The single was number one for a total of eight weeks.

Sammy Kaye recorded the song on the 31st March, 1941 and released it as an A side 78 single in 1941 on RCA Victor Records as 27391-A. The B side was "Two Hearts That Pass in the Night". Glenn Miller and his Orchestra also performed the song for radio broadcast the same year. Harry James also recorded a version in 1941 on Columbia 36171.

The lyrics are on the theme of a woman named Daisy who entreats her lover or husband to buy her fashionable luxury goods.

Jimmy Dorsey and His Orchestra with Bob Eberly and Helen O'Connell

"Green Eyes"

"Green Eyes" is a popular song, originally written in Spanish under the title "Aquellos Ojos Verdes" ("Those Green Eyes") by Adolfo Utrera and Nilo Menéndez, 1929. The English translation was made by Eddie Rivera and Eddie Woods in 1931.

The English version of the song was written in 1931 but did not become a major hit till ten years later when recorded by the Jimmy Dorsey orchestra. The recording was made on the 19th March, 1941 with vocals by Helen O'Connell and Bob Eberly and released by Decca Records as catalogue number 3698. The flip side was "Maria Elena." The record first reached the Billboard charts on the 9th May, 1941 and lasted 21 weeks on the chart, peaking at #1. Since "Maria Elena" was also a #1 hit, this was a major double-sided hit recording.

Jimmy Dorsey and His Orchestra with Bob Eberly

"Blue Champagne"

"Blue Champagne" is a song written by Grady Watts, Jimmy Eaton and Frank L. Ryerson and recorded by American bandleader Jimmy Dorsey with his orchestra, featuring vocals by singer Bob Eberly.

It was released by Decca Records in 1941, backed with "All Alone and Lonely". It topped The Billboard's National Best Selling Retail Records chart on the week of September 27, 1941, becoming Dorsey's fifth number-one single of that year.

It was released by Decca records as a 10 inch single.

Freddy Martin and His Orchestra

"Piano Concerto in B Flat"

"Piano Concerto in B Flat" Martin took his band into many prestigious hotels, including the Roosevelt Grill in New York City and the Ambassador Hotel in Los Angeles. A fixture on radio, his sponsored shows included NBC's Maybelline Penthouse Serenade of 1937. For Martin, real success came in 1941 with an arrangement from the first movement of Tchaikovsky's Piano Concerto No. 1 in B♭ minor. Reached number one on the 4th October, 1941 and stayed there for 7 weeks.

Martin recorded the piece instrumentally, but soon lyrics were put in and it was re-cut as "Tonight We Love" with Clyde Rogers' vocal – becoming his biggest hit. It sold over one million copies by 1946, and was awarded a gold disc by the RIAA.

Glenn Miller and His Orchestra with Tex Beneke and the Four Modernaires

"Chattanooga Choo Choo"

"Chattanooga Choo Choo" is a 1941 song written by Mack Gordon and composed by Harry Warren. It was originally recorded as a big band/swing tune by Glenn Miller and His Orchestra and featured in the 1941 movie Sun Valley Serenade. It was the first song to receive a gold record, presented by RCA Victor in 1942, for sales of 1.2 million copies.

The song was an extended production number in the 20th Century Fox film Sun Valley Serenade. The Glenn Miller recording, RCA Bluebird B-11230-R, became the #1 song on the 7th December, 1941, and remained at #1 for three weeks on the Billboard Best Sellers chart and again on the 27th December for a further two weeks. The flip side of the single was "I Know Why (And So Do You)", which was the A side.

Glenn Miller and His Orchestra with Ray Eberle and the Modernaires

"Elmer's Tune"

"Elmer's Tune" is a 1941 big band and jazz standard written by Elmer Albrecht, Dick Jurgens and Sammy Gallop. Glenn Miller and his Orchestra and Dick Jurgens and his Orchestra both charted with recordings of the composition. Glenn Miller had the most successful recording of the song. His version reached No. 1 on the Billboard charts. The popularity of the tune prompted Glenn Miller to ask Jurgens if he could record a vocal version of the song. Robbins Music Company, the song's publisher, hired Sammy Gallop to write the lyrics. Miller recorded his version of the song for RCA Bluebird (B-11274-A) on August 11, 1941 in New York with Ray Eberle on lead vocals and the Modernaires on backing vocals. This version was an even bigger success than Jurgens' recording, peaking at no.1 for one week on the Billboard Best Selling Retail Records chart for the week ending December 13, 1941, in a 20-week chart run.

Alton Glenn Miller was an American big-band trombonist, arranger, composer, and bandleader in the swing era. He was the best-selling recording artist from 1939 to 1942, leading one of the best-known big bands. Miller's recordings include "In the Mood", "Moonlight Serenade", "Pennsylvania 6-5000", "Chattanooga Choo Choo", "A String of Pearls", "At Last", "(I've Got a Gal In) Kalamazoo", "American Patrol", "Tuxedo Junction", "Elmer's Tune" and "Little Brown Jug". In just four years Glenn Miller scored 16 number-one records and 69 top ten hits—more than Elvis Presley (38 top 10s) and the Beatles (33 top 10s) did in their careers. While he was traveling to entertain U.S. troops in France during World War II, Miller's aircraft disappeared in bad weather over the English Channel.

WORLD EVENTS 1941

January

1st British naval officers were encouraged to search all captured ships for encoding machines and related paperwork.

2nd The United States announced plans to build 200 utilitarian freighters. These would come to be known as Liberty ships. Liberty ships were a class of cargo ship built in the United States during World War II. Though British in concept, the design was adapted by the United States for its simple, low-cost construction. Mass-produced on an unprecedented scale, the Liberty ship came to symbolize U.S. wartime industrial output.
The class was developed to meet British orders for transports to replace ships that had been lost. Eighteen American shipyards built 2,710 Liberty ships between 1941 and 1945 (an average of three ships every two days), easily the largest number of ships ever produced to a single design.

3rd The results of a Gallup poll were published asking Americans, "Do you think our country's future safety depends on England winning this war?" 68% said yes, 26% said no and 6% expressed no opinion.

4th Bugs Bunny was identified by name for the first time, in the short cartoon Elmer's Pet Rabbit.

6th U.S. President Franklin D. Roosevelt made the Four Freedoms speech during his State of the Union address. He proposed four fundamental freedoms that all the people of the world ought to enjoy: freedom of speech, freedom of worship, freedom from want and freedom from fear.

7th Japanese Admiral Isoroku Yamamoto presented Minister of the Navy Koshirō Oikawa with his ideas for a war against the United States in a memorandum titled Gumbi ni kansuru shiken (Views on Preparations for War). Yamamoto proposed a crippling first strike on American forces in the first few hours of the war, something that could best be accomplished by an air attack on the U.S. fleet at Pearl Harbour.

9th Hitler held a conference with his generals to discuss plans to attack the Soviet Union. Hitler said that German success in Russia would encourage Japan to attack the United States, thus keeping the Americans too occupied to get involved in the war in Europe.

10th The German civil administration in the Netherlands ordered the registration of all Jews in the country.

14th In New York City, brothers Anthony and William Esposito held up a man in a Fifth Avenue office building, shot him dead and then led police in a daytime chase through Manhattan. Both men were eventually apprehended, but not before a police officer was slain and a cab driver wounded in the throat. The trial would become one of the most famous insanity defence cases in history.

16th The Germans bombed Malta for the first time, killing 50 people, destroying 200 buildings and damaging the capital city of Valletta. The British aircraft carrier HMS Illustrious was hit and damaged again in Grand Harbour.

17th 23,190 people packed Madison Square Garden to watch Fritzie Zivic successfully defend the world welterweight boxing title against Henry Armstrong. The attendance is an all-time record for any of the different versions of the Garden.

Fritzie Zivic   **Henry Armstrong**

22nd British and Australian forces captured Tobruk and took 25,000 Italians prisoner.

23rd Charles Lindbergh came before the U.S. House Foreign Affairs Committee to oppose the Roosevelt Administration's Lend-Lease bill. Lindbergh testified that he would prefer to see "neither side win" in the war and hoped to see a "negotiated peace," and also expressed his belief that American entry into the war on Britain's side would still not be enough to defeat Germany without some kind of internal collapse.

30th Hitler gave a speech before 18,000 people at the Berlin Sportpalast on the eighth anniversary of the Nazis' coming to power. Hitler declared that any ship carrying aid to England within the range of German U-boats would be torpedoed, and also warned the United States that if anyone on the American continent tried to interfere in the European conflict, Germany's war aims would quickly change.

February

2nd | The British aircraft carrier HMS Formidable replaced the damaged Illustrious in the Mediterranean. The Illustrious was sent to the United States for repairs.

3rd | Erwin Rommel became head of the German military unit soon to be known as the Afrika Korps.

5th | Wendell Willkie ended his visit to England with a statement intended for the German people: "I am proud of my German blood, but I hate aggression and tyranny, and I now tell the German people that my convictions are fully shared by the overwhelming majority of Americans of German descent. They, too, believe in freedom and human rights. We German-Americans reject and hate aggression and the lust for power of the present German government."

7th | Operation Sonnenblume was the name given to the dispatch of German troops to North Africa in February 1941, during the Second World War. The Italian 10th Army had been destroyed by the British and Allied Western Desert Force attacks during Operation Compass (9th December 1940 – 9th February 1941). The first units of the new Deutsches Afrikakorps (DAK, Generalleutnant Erwin Rommel) departed Naples for Africa and arrived on the 11th February 1941.

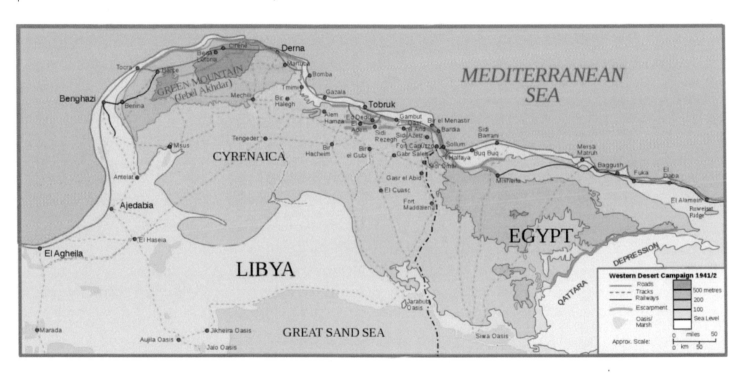

9th | British forces captured El Agheila. Winston Churchill halted the British advance in North Africa and began withdrawing troops to assist in the defence of Greece.

11th | Wendell Willkie, having returned from England, appeared before the Senate Foreign Relations Committee and urged that the United States provide Britain with five to ten destroyers a month.

14th | Kichisaburō Nomura came to the White House to present his credentials to President Roosevelt. The president told the ambassador that "there are developments in the relations between the United States and Japan which cause concern," and Nomura replied that he would do all he could to establish better understandings between the two nations.

February

15th | British and German troops engaged each other in North Africa for the first time in a skirmish near Sirte.

18th | Thousands of Australian troops arrived in Singapore to prepare the region for a possible attack by the Japanese.

23rd | Plutonium was chemically identified by Glenn T. Seaborg and his team of chemists at University of California, Berkeley.

24th | Hitler gave a speech in Munich on the 21st anniversary of the founding of the Nazi Party declaring that the U-boat offensive would intensify in the coming months.

25th | Operation Abstention was a code name given to a British invasion of the Italian island of Kastelorizo (Castellorizo) off the Turkish Aegean coast, during the Second World War, on the 25th February 1941. The goal was to establish a torpedo-boat base to challenge Italian naval and air supremacy on the Greek Dodecanese islands. The British landings were challenged by Italian land, air and naval forces, which forced the British troops to re-embark amidst some confusion and led to recriminations between the British commanders for underestimating the Italians.

26th | Franco belatedly replied to Hitler's three-week old letter, expressing support for the Axis but making exorbitant demands for the price of Spain's entry into the war.

27th | The 13th Academy Awards were held in Los Angeles, with Rebecca winning Best Picture. This year's ceremony marked the first time that the names of the winners were sealed in envelopes before they were opened during the ceremony itself, following the previous year's snafu when the Los Angeles Times published the winners ahead of the ceremony.

28th | Operation Abstention ended in Italian victory when the last remaining British commandos surrendered.

March

1st | Heinrich Himmler inspected the Auschwitz concentration camp and ordered it to be expanded to hold 30,000 prisoners.

March

4th   Operation Claymore was a British commando raid on the Norwegian Lofoten Islands during the Second World War. The Lofoten Islands were an important centre for the production of fish oil and glycerine, used in the German war economy. The landings were carried out on the 4th March 1941, by the men of No. 3 Commando, No. 4 Commando, a Royal Engineers section and 52 men from the Norwegian Independent Company 1. Supported by the 6th Destroyer Flotilla and two troop transports of the Royal Navy, the force made an unopposed landing and generally continued to meet no opposition. The original plan was to avoid contact with German forces and inflict the maximum of damage to German-controlled industry. They achieved their objective of destroying fish oil factories and some 3,600 t (3,500 long tons) of oil and glycerine. The British experienced only one accident; an officer injuring himself with his own revolver and returned with some 228 German prisoners, 314 loyal Norwegian volunteers and a number of Quisling regime collaborators. Through naval gunfire and demolition parties, 18,000 tons of shipping was sunk. Perhaps the most significant outcome of the raid was the capture of a set of rotor wheels for an Enigma machine and its code books from the German armed trawler Krebs. German naval codes could be read at Bletchley Park, providing the intelligence needed to allow Allied convoys to avoid U-boat concentrations.

6th   Winston Churchill issued the Battle of the Atlantic directive, creating a committee to oversee the logistics of that theatre. The Battle of the Atlantic was the longest continuous military campaign in World War II, running from 1939 to the defeat of Nazi Germany in 1945, and was a major part of the Naval history of World War II. At its core was the Allied naval blockade of Germany, announced the day after the declaration of war, and Germany's subsequent counter-blockade. It was at its height from mid-1940 through to the end of 1943.

9th   German aircraft bombed London and damaged Buckingham Palace. The Café de Paris nightclub was also heavily damaged and did not re-open until after the war.

10th   Beer was rationed in Vichy France due to a shortage of barley and hops. Starting on the 15th March, beer could not be sold on Saturdays or Tuesdays.

11th   Bronko Nagurski defeated Ray Steele to reclaim the National Wrestling Association World Heavyweight Championship.

16th   A fire broke out on the docked German ocean liner SS Bremen, causing such extensive damage that the ship would be scrapped. Initially thought to be the work of raiders, the arsonist was later said to have been a cabin boy avenging a punishment.

March

17th German submarine U-99 was scuttled southeast of Iceland after being severely damaged by the British destroyers Walker and Vanoc. This was the first successful use of radar by surface units against U-boats, a factor in the ending of Germany's First Happy Time.

19th Rommel met with Hitler, Walther von Brauchitsch and Franz Halder. Rommel was told he could expect no reinforcements in Libya until May when he would receive the 15th Panzer Division.

20th U.S. Under Secretary of State Sumner Welles warned the Soviet ambassador to Washington Konstantin Umansky that the United States had information confirming Germany's intention to attack the Soviet Union.

27th The Yugoslav coup d'état occurred. Dušan Simović and other Serb nationalist officers in the Royal Yugoslav Air Force overthrew Yugoslavia's pro-Axis government and intended to back out of the Tripartite Pact. When Hitler learned of the coup he issued Directive No. 25 ordering an invasion of Yugoslavia.

28th Hitler awarded Hanna Reitsch the Iron Cross Second Class, making her the first woman of the war to receive the medal. Hanna Reitsch was a German aviatrix and test pilot. During the Nazi era, she and Melitta von Stauffenberg flight tested many of the regime's new aircraft. She set more than 40 flight altitude records and women's endurance records in gliding and unpowered flight, before and after World War II.

29th Wisconsin defeated Washington State 39–34 in the championship game of the NCAA Men's Division I Basketball Tournament.

30th Hitler held a conference with his generals in whom he said that the upcoming war with Russia would be a race war in which communist commissars and Jews would be exterminated by SS Einsatzgruppen following behind the advancing armies. Hitler expected the Soviet Union to be defeated in a matter of weeks and declared, "We have only to kick in the door and the whole rotten structure will come crashing down."

31st 109 RAF bombers attacked the German warships Scharnhorst and Gneisenau in Brest, France, but were unable to score any hits.

April

1st | The Royal Air Force dropped the first 4,000-pound blockbuster bombs of the war, by Vickers Wellington medium bombers in a raid over Emden.

2nd | During one of his radio broadcasts, the anonymous pro-Nazi commentator derisively nicknamed Lord Haw-Haw confirmed his identity as William Joyce.

4th | The naval battle known as the Action of 4 April 1941 was fought in the mid-Atlantic Ocean. The German commerce raider Thor sank the British auxiliary cruiser Voltaire.

6th | At 1:30 a.m. in Moscow, the Soviet Union and the new government of Yugoslavia signed a treaty of friendship and non-aggression. The treaty was backdated to April 5, possibly in anticipation of a German attack and the Russians wanting to avoid any impression that the agreement was signed while Yugoslavia was at war.

7th | On Budget Day in the United Kingdom, Chancellor of the Exchequer Kingsley Wood presented an innovative plan modelled after Keynesian economics that used taxation and forced savings to attack an estimated £500 million "inflation gap". Wood increased taxes by £250 million and projected a deficit of £2.304 billion, almost identical to the previous year's deficit of £2.475 billion. British newspaper editorials generally found the wartime sacrifices asked for in the budget to be reasonable and the stock exchange also took the news of the budget well.

9th | Winston Churchill made a lengthy speech before the House of Commons reviewing the course of the war. He said in conclusion: "Once we have gained the Battle of the Atlantic and are sure of the constant flow of American supplies which are being prepared for us, then, however far Hitler may go or whatever new millions and scores of millions he may lap in misery, we who are armed with the sword of retributive justice shall be on his track."

13th | Soviet–Japanese Neutrality Pact: Japan and the Soviet Union signed a five-year Treaty of Neutrality, pledging to remain neutral in the event of one country being attacked by a third party. The pact also saw the Soviet Union recognize du jure Manchukuo for the first time.

16th | The Battle of the Tarigo Convoy was a naval battle of World War II, part of the Battle of the Mediterranean. It was fought on the 16th April 1941, between four British and three Italian destroyers, near the Kerkennah Islands off Sfax, in the Tunisian coast. The battle was named after the Italian flagship, the destroyer Luca Tarigo. Control of the sea between Italy and Libya was heavily disputed as both sides sought to safeguard their own convoys while interdicting those of their opponent. Axis convoys to North Africa supplied the German and Italian armies there, and British attacks were based on Malta, itself dependent upon convoys.

18th | The Messerschmitt Me 262 prototype had its first test flight, although only with a piston engine at first.

19th | A night-time German air-raid on London killed 13 firefighters, the largest single loss of firefighters in British history.

20th | The British cargo liner Empire Endurance was torpedoed and sunk west of Rockall by the German submarine U-73.

April

23rd | The results of a Gallup poll were published asking Americans, "If it appears certain that Britain will be defeated unless we use part of our navy to protect ships going to Britain, would you favour or oppose such convoys?" 71% expressed favour, 21% were opposed and 8% expressed no opinion.

27th | Winston Churchill made a radio broadcast reporting on the war situation. "When I spoke to you early in February many people believed the Nazi boastings that the invasion of Britain was about to begin. Now it has not begun yet, and with every week that passes we grow stronger on the sea, in the air and in the number, quality, training and equipment of the great armies that now guard our island," Churchill said. Returning to the line in that February speech asking for the "tools" to "finish the job," Churchill said that "that is what it now seems the Americans are going to do. And that is why I feel a very strong conviction that though the Battle of the Atlantic will be long and hard and its issue is by no means yet determined; it has entered upon a grimmer but at the same time a far more favourable phase."

28th | Another Gallup poll result was released asking Americans, "If you were asked to vote today on the question of the United States entering the war against Germany and Italy, how would you vote — to go into the war, or to stay out of the war?" 81% said stay out, a 7 percent decrease since the same question was polled in January. Another question asked, "If it appeared certain that there was no other way to defeat Germany and Italy except for the United States to go to war against them, would you be in favour of the United States going to war?" 68% said yes, 24% said no, and 8% expressed no opinion.

29th | The British passenger ship City of Nagpur was torpedoed and sunk in the Atlantic Ocean by the German submarine U-75.

30th | The troop transport Nerissa was torpedoed and sunk by German submarine U-552. Nerissa was the only transport carrying Canadian troops to be lost during the war.

May

1st | The Ministry of War Transport (MoWT) was a department of the British Government formed early in the Second World War to control transportation policy and resources. It was formed by merging the Ministry of Shipping and the Ministry of Transport, bringing responsibility for both shipping and land transport to a single department, and easing problems of co-ordination of transport in wartime. The MoWT was founded on the 1st May 1941, when Lord Leathers was appointed Minister of War Transport. Following the general election of July 1945, Alfred Barnes was appointed Minister of War Transport, remaining in the post after the department was renamed the Ministry of Transport in April 1946.

4th | Adolf Hitler made an address to the Reichstag reviewing the Balkan campaign and declaring that the German Reich and its allies were superior to any conceivable coalition in the world.

6th | The Greenock Blitz is the name given to two nights of intensive bombing of the town of Greenock, Scotland by the Nazi German Luftwaffe during the Second World War. The raids over the nights of the 6th and 7th .May 1941 targeted the shipyards and berthed ships around the town (similar to the Clydebank Blitz the previous March). The brunt of the bombing fell on residential areas. Over the two nights, 271 people were killed and over 10,200 injured. From a total of 180,000 homes nearly 25,000 suffered damage and 5,000 were destroyed outright

May

7th | The German weather ship München was captured near Iceland. Secret papers were found on board that improved the British understanding of the Enigma coding machines.

8th | Nottingham was the first city in Britain to develop an ARP (Air Raid Precautions) network. It was developed because of the foresight of Nottingham City Police Chief Constable Captain Athelstan Popkess. The city was divided into zones, controlled by report and control centres with 45 auxiliary fire service stations.
By the time of the raid, Nottingham had built a significant number of public shelters. The John Player & Sons tobacco company had built a network of tunnels at its factory and under local streets sufficient to house around 5,000 of its workers. The raid on the night of the 8th – 9th May by the Luftwaffe was targeted at Nottingham and Derby. The X-Gerät beams set up to cover the Rolls Royce works were detected, and radio counter-measures diverted the attack to the moors north east of the town.
A Starfish decoy fire system located near Cropwell Butler in the Vale of Belvoir confused the aircraft, and many of the bombs intended for Nottingham were dropped on open farmland in the vale

9th | The Luftwaffe attempted to hit the Rolls-Royce aero engine factory in the East Midlands, but their bombs only managed to kill a few farm animals.

10th | Deputy Führer Rudolf Hess flew a Messerschmitt Bf 110 to Scotland on a solo peace mission, parachuting into Eaglesham near his objective of Dungavel House after running out of fuel.

12th | The Nazi Party issued a press release on the subject of Rudolf Hess, claiming that he was "suffering from mental illness" and that the Führer had ordered the immediate arrest of those who helped Hess.

14th | The first mass round-up of Jews in Paris took place. More than 3,700 foreign Jews were arrested when they reported to a gymnasium for police examination of their status. They were sent to the internment camps of Pithiviers and Beaune-la-Rolande.

15th | The British attempted to keep the Nazis guessing as to what Rudolf Hess had told them by having Labour Minister Ernest Bevin say in the government's first official statement on the matter: "I do not believe that Hitler did not know that Hess was coming to England. From my point of view Hess is a murderer. He is no man I would ever negotiate with and I don't change even for diplomatic reasons. I am not going to be deceived."

May

18th	Operation Rheinübung ("Exercise Rhine") was the sortie into the Atlantic by the new German battleship Bismarck and heavy cruiser Prinz Eugen on 18th – 27th May 1941, during World War II. This operation to block Allied shipping to the United Kingdom culminated with the sinking of Bismarck.
21st	The Central Committee War Section met in Moscow. Joseph Stalin dismissed intelligence indicating a German attack on the Soviet Union was imminent, believing it was misinformation from the British trying to draw the Soviet Union into the war. When the head of Soviet intelligence argued with Stalin he was arrested and shot.
22nd	The British cruisers Fiji and Gloucester and the destroyer Greyhound were all bombed and sunk by the Luftwaffe around Crete.

HMS Fiji **HMS Gloucester** **HMS Greyhound**

23rd	Vichy Vice-Premier François Darlan made a radio broadcast to the French people denying that he was ever asked to hand over the French Navy or any colonial territory during his recent conversations with Hitler. "France freely is choosing the road she is taking," Darlan stated. "On her depends her present and her future? She will have the peace which she makes herself. She will have the place in the organization of Europe which she will have made for herself."
24th	The Battle of the Denmark Strait was a naval engagement on the 24th May 1941 in the Second World War, between ships of the Royal Navy and the German Kriegsmarine. The British battleship HMS Prince of Wales and the battlecruiser HMS Hood fought the German battleship Bismarck and the heavy cruiser Prinz Eugen, which were attempting to break out into the North Atlantic to attack Allied merchant shipping. Less than 10 minutes after the British opened fire, a shell from Bismarck struck Hood near her aft ammunition magazines. Soon afterwards, Hood exploded and sank within three minutes, with the loss of all but three of her crew. Prince of Wales continued to exchange fire with Bismarck but suffered serious malfunctions in her main armament. The British battleship had only just been completed in late March 1941, and used new quadruple gun turrets that were unreliable. Therefore, Prince of Wales soon broke off the engagement. The battle was considered a tactical victory for the Germans but its impact was short-lived. The damage done to Bismarck's forward fuel tanks forced the abandonment of the breakout and an attempt to escape to dry dock facilities in occupied France, producing an operational victory for the British. Incensed by the loss of Hood, a large British force pursued and sank Bismarck three days later.
26th	The last battle of the battleship Bismarck began in the Atlantic Ocean. That morning a British Catalina reconnaissance aircraft spotted the Bismarck. Starting at dusk, ships and aircraft of the Royal Navy and Royal Air Force attacked the battleship with torpedoes. A hit from a Fairey Swordfish torpedo bomber flown by John Moffatt damaged the Bismarck's rudder.

May

27th After taking more damage, the crippled Bismarck was scuttled to avoid being captured by the enemy.

28th Nazi Germany and Vichy France signed the Paris Protocols, granting the Germans military facilities in French colonies in exchange for the French receiving a reduction in the occupation costs they were obligated to pay Germany as well as the release of French prisoners of war. The agreement would never be ratified.

29th The British destroyer HMS Imperial was scuttled in the Mediterranean northeast of Bardia after being bombed and heavily damaged by Italian aircraft.

30th Floyd Davis and Mauri Rose won the Indianapolis 500. This was the last time in Indianapolis 500 history that one winning car would carry two different drivers. The race would not be held again until 1946.

31st An armistice was signed in the Anglo-Iraqi War.

June

2nd Adolf Hitler and Benito Mussolini met at the Brenner Pass once again. During the five-hour conference Hitler ranted about Rudolf Hess and other recent events, but kept Mussolini in the dark about the upcoming invasion of the Soviet Union. However, major Italian troop movements in the Balkans around this time suggest that the Italian government was likely aware of Hitler's intentions anyway. Mussolini reportedly told Count Ciano after the meeting, "I wouldn't be at all sorry if Germany in her war with Russia got her feathers plucked."

4th British intelligence intercepted Ambassador Ōshima's coded message which included considerable details of Germany's plan to attack the USSR. However, due to a lack of either translators or interest, the report was not delivered to the Joint Intelligence Committee for eight days.

5th United States landed 4,000 marines in Iceland to replace the British garrison.

6th The Commissar Order was an order issued by the German High Command (OKW) on the 6th June 1941 before Operation Barbarossa. Its official name was Guidelines for the Treatment of Political Commissars. It instructed the Wehrmacht that any Soviet political commissar identified among captured troops be summarily executed as a purported enforcer of the "Judeo-Bolshevism" ideology in military forces. It is one of a series of criminal orders issued by the leadership.

7th Whirlaway won the Belmont Stakes and completed the U.S. Triple Crown of Thoroughbred Racing.

9th The funeral of ex-kaiser Wilhelm II was held in Doorn. Although Hitler had wanted a state funeral in Berlin with himself in a prominent role, Wilhelm's family insisted on respecting instructions he'd given in 1933 that he was to be buried in Doorn if Germany was not a monarchy at the time of his death. However, a delegation of Nazi officials led by Arthur Seyss-Inquart was allowed to attend as well as a Wehrmacht guard of honour, and Wilhelm's wishes that Nazi regalia not be displayed at his funeral were ignored.

10th On the first anniversary of Italy's entry into the war, Mussolini said in a speech to the Grand Council of Fascism that the United States was already in a de facto state of war with the Axis, but that "America's attitude does not bother us excessively ... American intervention would merely lengthen the war and would not save England."

15th Operation Battle-axe was a British Army operation during the Second World War on the 15th June 1941, to clear eastern Cyrenaica of German and Italian forces and raise the Siege of Tobruk. It was the first time during the war that a significant German force fought on the defensive. The British lost over half of their tanks on the first day and only one of three attacks succeeded. The British achieved mixed results on the second day, being pushed back on their western flank and repulsing a big German counter-attack in the centre. On the third day, the British narrowly avoided disaster by withdrawing just ahead of a German encircling movement. The failure of Battle-axe led to the replacement of British General Sir Archibald Wavell, Commander-in-Chief Middle East, by Claude Auchinleck; Wavell took Auchinleck's position as Commander-in-Chief, India.

17th The British called off the failed Operation Battle-axe after taking 1,000 casualties and losing almost 100 tanks.

18th Joe Louis retained the World Heavyweight Championship of boxing with a thirteenth-round knockout of Billy Conn at the Polo Grounds in New York City.

19th Germany and Italy ordered the United States to close all 31 of its consulates in retaliation for President Roosevelt's order of three days earlier.

20th The American submarine O-9 foundered during a test dive off Portsmouth, New Hampshire. All 33 crew were lost.

21st Hitler sent Benito Mussolini a secret message informing him of the German invasion of the Soviet Union. "I waited until this moment, Duce, to send you this information, it is because the final decision itself will not be made until 7 o'clock tonight," Hitler wrote. "I earnestly beg you, therefore, to refrain, above all, from making any explanation to your Ambassador at Moscow, for there is no absolute guarantee that our coded reports cannot be decoded. I, too, shall wait until the last moment to have my own Ambassador informed of the decisions reached."

22nd Hitler issued a lengthy proclamation of war with the Soviet Union presenting his justification for the German invasion. As usual, Hitler presented himself as doing everything he could to preserve peace and only turning to force as a last resort.

22nd Winston Churchill gave a speech announcing the German invasion of the Soviet Union and explaining Britain's new alliance with Russia. "No one has been a more consistent opponent of Communism than I have for the last twenty-five years," Churchill said. "I will unsay no word that I have spoken about it. But all this fades away before the spectacle which is now unfolding ... Any man or state that fights on against Nazidom will have our aid. Any man or state who marches with Hitler is our foe ... It follows, therefore, that we shall give whatever help we can to Russia and the Russian people. We shall appeal to all our friends and allies in every part of the world to take the same course and pursue it, as we shall, faithfully and steadfastly to the end."

24th British cargo ship Brockley Hill was torpedoed and sunk off Cape Farewell, Greenland by German submarine U-651.

25th The Kaunas pogrom was a massacre of Jews living in Kaunas, Lithuania that took place on the 25th – 29th June 1941 – the first days of the Operation Barbarossa and of Nazi occupation of Lithuania. The most infamous incident occurred in the Lietūkis garage, where several dozen Jewish men were publicly tortured and executed on the 27th June; most of them killed by a single club-wielding assailant nicknamed the "Death Dealer." After June, systematic executions took place at various forts of the Kaunas Fortress, especially the Seventh and Ninth Fort.

26th The bombing of Kassa took place on the 26th June 1941, when still unidentified aircraft conducted an airstrike on the city of Kassa, then a part of Hungary, today Košice in Slovakia. This attack became the pretext for the government of Hungary to declare war on the Soviet Union the next day, 27th June. On the 26th June 1941, four days after Germany attacked the Soviet Union in violation of the Molotov–Ribbentrop non-aggression treaty as a part of Operation Barbarossa, three unidentified planes bombed the city, killing and wounding over a dozen people and causing minor material damage. Numerous buildings were hit, including the local post and telegraph office. Hours after the attack, the Hungarian cabinet "passed a resolution calling for the declaration of the existence of a state of war between Hungary and the USSR.

28th The German weather ship Lauenburg was intercepted by British warships north of Iceland. A boarding party from the destroyer HMS Tartar seized a large amount of material that would be useful in cracking German codes, and then the Lauenburg was sunk by gunfire.

29th 212,000 children were evacuated from Leningrad.

30th The Battle of Brody was a tank battle fought between the 1st Panzer Group's III Army Corps and XLVIII Army Corps (Motorized) and five mechanized corps of the Soviet 5th Army and 6th Army in the triangle formed by the towns of Dubno, Lutsk, and Brody between 23rd and 30th June 1941. It is known in Soviet historiography as a part of the "border defensive battles". Although the Red Army formations inflicted heavy losses on the German forces, they were outmanoeuvred and suffered enormous losses in tanks. Poor Soviet logistics, German air supremacy as well as a total breakdown in Red Army command and control ensured victory for the Wehrmacht despite overwhelming Red Army numerical and technological superiority. This was one of the most intense armoured engagements in the opening phase of Operation Barbarossa and recent scholarship considers it the largest tank battle of World War II, surpassing the more famous Battle of Prokhorovka. Ended with German victory.

1st | Joe DiMaggio of the New York Yankees tied the 44-year old hitting streak record of Wee Willie Keeler by hitting safely in both games of a doubleheader against the Boston Red Sox, extending the streak to 44 consecutive games. He took the record to 56 games and that record still stands today.

Joe DiMaggio   **Wee Willie Keeler**

3rd | The Battle of Białystok–Minsk ended in German victory. 290,000 Soviet troops with 2,500 tanks surrendered in the Białystok pocket.

4th | U.S. President Franklin D. Roosevelt made an Independence Day broadcast warning that "the United States will never survive as a happy and fertile oasis of liberty surrounded by a cruel desert of dictatorship. And so it is that when we repeat the great pledge to our country and to our flag, it must be our deep conviction that we pledge as well our work, our will, and, if it be necessary, our very lives."

7th | Winston Churchill sent a letter to Stalin saying that there was "genuine admiration" in Britain for the "bravery and tenacity of the soldiers and the people" of the Soviet Union. Churchill also pledged, "We shall do everything to help you that time, geography and our growing resources allow." Stalin was unimpressed by the vagueness of the letter and responded by asking for a formal agreement, since he wanted to ensure that Britain would not stand aside while Germany and the Soviet Union destroyed each other.

9th | A brief discussion was held in the British House of Commons about the arrangement by the Nazis for P. G. Wodehouse to give weekly radio broadcasts from Germany to the United States. Foreign Affairs Secretary Anthony Eden said he would take into consideration the suggestion from Geoffrey Mander "to bring to the attention of Mr. Wodehouse and others the grave peril in which they place themselves by playing the Nazi game during the war."

10th | Stalin received a reply from Churchill accepting his request to work on reaching a formal agreement.

The Anglo-Soviet Agreement was a formal military alliance signed by the United Kingdom and the Soviet Union against Germany on the 12th July 1941; shortly after the German invasion of the latter. Both powers pledged to assist each other and not make separate peace with Germany. Military alliance was to be valid for the duration of war and agreement was replaced by the Anglo-Soviet Treaty of 1942.

17th | The Twin Pimples Raid was a British Commando raid on a feature in the Italian lines during the siege of Tobruk in the Second World War. The raid, carried out by men of the No. 8 (Guards) Commando and the Royal Australian Engineers, was a complete success. However it did not end the siege; that continued until November 1941, when the Allied advance during Operation Crusader reached the town.

18th | Stalin wrote to Churchill again saying, "It seems to me that the military position of the Soviet Union, as well as that of Great Britain, would be considerably improved if there could be established a front against Hitler in the West- Northern France, and in the North- the Arctic."

20th | Churchill wrote back to Stalin explaining that opening a new front in the west was presently out of the question. "To attempt a landing in force would be to encounter a bloody repulse, and petty raids would only lead to fiascos doing far more harm than good to both of us", Churchill wrote. "You must remember that we have been fighting alone for more than a year, and that, though our resources are growing, and will grow fast from now on, we are at the utmost strain both at home and in the Middle East by land and air, and also that the Battle of the Atlantic, on which our life depends, and the movement of all our convoys in the teeth of the U-boat and Fokke-Wulf blockade, strains our naval resources, great though they may be, to the utmost limit." Churchill did agree to conduct air and sea operations in the north to attack enemy shipping.

24th | Some 700 employees of the Alcan aluminium company went on strike in Arvida, Quebec, Canada. Since the industry had been classified as essential to the war effort, the strike was illegal.

25th | An executive order by President Roosevelt froze Japanese assets in the United States. At Chiang Kai-shek's request, the order was extended to Chinese assets as well.

26th | Britain followed the United States in imposing economic sanctions on Japan and freezing all Japanese assets in areas under their control. Japan retaliated by freezing all U.S. and British assets in return.

27th | Operation Chess was a British Commando raid during the Second World War. It was carried out by 17 men of No. 12 Commando commanded by a Second Lieutenant Pinckney over the night of 27th /28th July 1941. The target for the raid was Ambleteuse, Pas-de-Calais, France. The raiding party were towed across the English Channel in two Landing Craft by a Motor Launch. This cast them off two miles from the Slack River near Ambleteuse. They remained ashore for one hour, no prisoners were taken. Cdr. Sir Geoffrey Congreve Bt DSO died of his wounds received during the raid.

29th | The Arvida strike ended when the Canadian government amended the Defence of Canada Regulations to allow the Minister of National Defence to call out troops to deal with labour disputes without requiring permission from municipal or provincial authorities. A subsequent royal commission concluded that while the strike was illegal, it was caused by workers' frustrations over salaries and working conditions rather than subversives as Munitions and Supply Minister C. D. Howe had claimed.

30th | The British mine-laying submarine HMS Cachalot was rammed and sunk in the Mediterranean Sea by the Italian torpedo boat Generale Achille Papa.

31st | Ludwig Crüwell was put in overall charge of the Afrika Korps, while Erwin Rommel took control of the newly created Panzer Armee Afrika.

August

1st U.S. President Franklin D. Roosevelt announced an embargo on the export of oil and aviation fuel to anywhere outside the Western Hemisphere with the exception of the British Empire. This action was aimed at Japan.

3rd The German Catholic Bishop Clemens August Graf von Galen gave a sermon condemning the Nazi practice of euthanasia. Thousands of copies of the sermon were distributed throughout Germany, breaking the secrecy that surrounded the euthanasia programme known as Aktion T4.

4th Adolf Hitler met with Fedor von Bock, Heinz Guderian and Hermann Hoth. All three generals agreed that a drive on Moscow should be top priority and could commence as early as the 20th August, but Hitler favoured other objectives such as the elimination of enemy pockets.

6th In the British House of Commons, British Foreign Secretary Anthony Eden warned Japan that any action threatening the independence and integrity of Thailand would be "of immediate concern" to the British government. U.S. Secretary of State Cordell Hull mirrored those statements that same day when he said at a press conference that any move by Japan into Thailand would be a matter of concern to the United States.

7th U.S. President Franklin D. Roosevelt arrived at Placentia Bay, Newfoundland aboard the heavy cruiser USS Augusta, ostensibly on vacation but actually to hold a conference with Winston Churchill.

9th British fighter ace Douglas Bader was forced to bail out of his damaged Spitfire Mk VA over northern France in controversial circumstances and was captured. Some accounts have his plane being involved in a mid-air collision with a Bf 109, but it is also possible he was shot down or was a victim of friendly fire.

Douglas Bader

Spitfire Mk VA

BF 109

10th President Roosevelt and his representatives came aboard the Prince of Wales for a Sunday prayer service with Churchill, who later recalled the event as "a deeply moving expression of the unity of faith of our two peoples." Churchill selected the hymns himself, ending with "Our God, Our Help in Ages Past".

12th The Royal Air Force conducted the heaviest daylight bombing raid against Germany since the war began. The Germans could not offer as much opposition as they once did because many of their planes had been diverted to the Eastern Front.

14th Franklin D. Roosevelt and Winston Churchill jointly issued the Atlantic Charter, stating the Allied goals for the post-war world.

August

15th | Roosevelt and Churchill sent a joint message of assistance to the Soviet Union. "We realize fully how vitally important to the defeat of Hitlerism is the brave and steadfast resistance of the Soviet Union and we feel therefore that we must not in any circumstances fail to act quickly and immediately in this matter on planning the program for the future allocation of our joint resources," the statement concluded.

16th | The Germans occupied the important Soviet naval base at Mykolaiv and captured warships, ammunition and repair facilities.

18th | The Nazis arrested over 300 Swing Kids in Hamburg. Most were sent home and some had their long hair cut as punishment, but the suspected leaders of the swing youth were imprisoned in concentration camps or sent to the front lines.

20th | The second mass round-up of Jews in Paris began at the request of the Gestapo's Jewish Affairs Department. Over the next five days a total of 4,232 Jews were arrested.

21st | In revenge for the execution two days earlier of the French Resistance member Samuel Tyszelman, communist activist Pierre Georges assassinated German naval cadet Alfons Moser at the Barbès – Rochechouart metro station in Paris by shooting him in the back. This marked the beginning of a cycle of assassinations by Resistance fighters and retribution from authorities that would claim hundreds of lives.

22nd | A German order signed by Otto von Stülpnagel decreed that in response to the previous day's assassination of a member of the German Armed Forces, all Frenchmen detained by or on behalf of German authorities would be considered as hostages. If any further incident occurred, a number of these hostages were to be shot.

23rd | Canadian Prime Minister William Lyon Mackenzie King made a speech to 10,000 Canadian troops in Aldershot, England. Some of the soldiers, tired of endless training exercises and anxious to see some action, booed and heckled the Prime Minister.

24th | Winston Churchill broadcast a message to the world about his recent meeting with President Roosevelt and the signing of the Atlantic Charter. Churchill explained that the Charter differed from the attitude adopted by the Allies in the latter part of World War I because it did not assume that there would never be any war again, and "that instead of trying to ruin German trade by all kinds of additional trade barriers and hindrances, as was the mood of 1917, we have definitely adopted the view that it is not in the interests of the world and of our two countries that any large nation should be unprosperous or shut out from the means of making a decent living for itself and its people by its industry and enterprise."

28th | The German submarine U-570 was beached and captured at Þorlákshöfn, Iceland after being forced to the surface by depth charges from a Lockheed Hudson of 269 Squadron the day before. The British would put the submarine back into service as HMS Graph.

30th | Operation Acid Drop was a British Commando raid during the Second World War. This was the first commando raid carried out by No. 5 Commando and consisted of two simultaneous operations over the night of 30th /31st August 1941. Each raid consisted of one officer and 14 men, their targets were the beaches at Hardelot and Merlimont in the Pas-de-Calais, France with the aim of carrying out reconnaissance and if possible, to capture a German soldier. It was a hit and run type raid with only 30 minutes ashore but in the event neither party encountered any Germans.

September

1st U.S. President Franklin D. Roosevelt gave a Labor Day radio address to the American people. "American labour now bears a tremendous responsibility in the winning of this most brutal, most terrible of all wars," the president said. "In our factories and shops and arsenals we are building weapons on a scale great in its magnitude. To all the battle fronts of this world these weapons are being dispatched, by day and by night, over the seas and through the air. And this Nation is now devising and developing new weapons of unprecedented power toward the maintenance of democracy ... Our vast effort, and the unity of purpose that inspires that effort, are due solely to our recognition of the fact that our fundamental rights - including the rights of labour — are threatened by Hitler's violent attempt to rule the world."

3rd Zyklon B was used experimentally at Auschwitz concentration camp, gassing 600 Soviet prisoners of war and 250 sick Polish prisoners. The experiment was deemed a success.

7th The results of a Gallup poll were published asking Americans, "Should the United States take steps now to keep Japan from becoming more powerful, even if it means risking a war with Japan?" 70% said yes, 18% said no and 12% expressed no opinion.

11th Charles Lindbergh made a speech on behalf of the America First Committee in Des Moines, Iowa which included remarks that would be instantly controversial: "The three most important groups who have been pressing this country toward war are the British, the Jewish and the Roosevelt administration." Lindbergh said he admired the British and Jewish races, but claimed that the Jews' "greatest danger to this country lies in their large ownership and influence in our motion pictures, our press, our radio and our government."

14th The U.S. Navy provided escorts for British convoy Hx 150, the first time that the Americans took a direct part in the North Atlantic campaign.

17th The British government ordered potatoes to be sold at 1d so people would eat more of them.

19th The Germans captured Kiev and took 500,000 Red Army soldiers prisoner.

20th Allied convoy SC 44 was attacked in the North Atlantic by Wolfpack Brandenburg. The CAM ship SS Empire Burton was sunk by U-74 and the cargo ship Pink Star and tanker T.J. Williams were sunk by U-552.

22nd "Russian Tank Week" began in the United Kingdom. From this day through September 26, all armoured vehicles produced in Britain were to be delivered to the Soviets.

25th The war film A Yank in the R.A.F. starring Tyrone Power and Betty Grable had its world premiere at Grauman's Chinese Theatre in Hollywood.

26th The Congressional hearings on allegations of propaganda in American films adjourned with the intention to resume in January 1942. The media was almost universally critical of the attacks made on the film industry during the hearings, as the isolationist Senators who initiated the proceedings came across as anti-Semitic and more paranoid about Hollywood than any threat from Hitler.

30th The Germans launched Operation Typhoon, the assault on Moscow, when Heinz Guderian's forces attacked along the Bryansk Front.

October

1st | The Moscow Conference ended. The United States agreed to supply the Soviets with $1 billion worth of arms and equipment.

2nd | Adolf Hitler issued a message to the German troops on the Eastern Front declaring, "Today begins the last great, decisive battle of this year."

3rd | Hitler made a public speech at the Berlin Sportpalast, his first since the German invasion of the Soviet Union began. Hitler declared that Russia was "to a great extent" already destroyed and that Germany had the capability to "beat all possible enemies" no matter "how many billions they are going to spend," a remark that appeared to be directed at the United States.

4th | Norwegians were warned by their German occupiers that they would face starvation if anti-Nazi unrest continued.

8th | U.S. President Franklin D. Roosevelt sent Stalin a short message stating that he was "confident that ways will be found to provide the material and supplies necessary to fight Hitler on all fronts, including your own. I want particularly to take this occasion to express my great confidence that your armies will ultimately prevail over Hitler and to assure you of our great determination to give any possible material assistance."

9th | President Roosevelt asked Congress for immediate authority to arm American merchant ships. "We will not let Hitler prescribe the waters of the world which our ships may travel," the president said. "The American flag is not going to be driven from the seas either by his submarines, his airplanes or his threats."

11th | President Roosevelt wrote to Winston Churchill requesting a gentleman's agreement to share information on atomic research. Churchill would write back in December accepting the request.

12th | On the 12th October 1941 at the orders of Hans Krueger thousands of Jews gathered at the Ringplatz market square for a "selection". The Nazi forces escorted them to the Jewish cemetery, where the mass graves had already been prepared. On the way, the Ukrainian and German guards beat and tortured the prisoners. At the cemetery the Jews were forced to give away their valuables, and show their papers. Some were released. The shooters ordered the Jews gathered in groups to strip naked and then proceed to the graves. The men of the Sicherheitspolizei (SiPo) were the first to open fire, augmented by members of the Nürnberg Order Police, and the Bahnschutz railroad police. The victims either fell into the graves or were ordered to jump in before being killed. Between 10,000 and 12,000 Jews were murdered: men, women and children.

15th | Most of the Soviet government evacuated Moscow, although Stalin remained in the capital.

19th | Joseph Stalin proclaimed a state of siege in the capital and issued an Order of the Day that "Moscow will be defended to the last."

21st | The comic book superhero Wonder Woman made her first appearance in All Star Comics issue #8.

22nd | 27 French hostages were shot outside Châteaubriant in reprisal for the killing of a German soldier in Nantes two days previously.

October

23rd The British destroyer HMS Cossack was torpedoed and damaged in the Atlantic Ocean by the German submarine U-563. The Cossack tried to return to Gibraltar for repairs but would sink in bad weather four days later.

25th President Roosevelt released a formal statement condemning reprisal executions carried out by the Nazis in occupied Europe. "The practice of executing scores of innocent hostages in reprisal for isolated attacks on Germans in countries temporarily under the Nazi heel revolts a world already inured to suffering brutality," the statement read.

27th President Roosevelt made an address on Navy Day declaring that "America has been attacked," referring to the Kearny incident ten days earlier. "I say that we do not propose to take this lying down. Our determination not to take it lying down has been expressed in the orders to the American Navy to shoot on sight. Those orders stand." The president also that "when we have helped to end the curse of Hitlerism we shall help to establish a new peace which will give to decent people everywhere a better chance to live and prosper in security and in freedom and in faith. Each day that passes we are producing and providing more and more arms for the men who are fighting on actual battle-fronts. That is our primary task." Palestinian leader Amin al-Husseini arrived in Rome for talks with Fascist leaders.

29th Winston Churchill gives his famous "Never Give In" speech at Harrow School.

30th The Royal Air Force bombed the German naval supply base at Ålesund, Norway.

31st While escorting Allied convoy HX 156 in the North Atlantic, the American destroyer USS Reuben James was sunk by the German submarine U-552 with the loss of 115 of 159 crew.

November

1st A formal statement from Adolf Hitler claimed that the United States "has attacked Germany" and that Roosevelt had been placed before the "tribunal" for world judgment. Germany disputed the American account of the sinking of the Reuben James and claimed that a German submarine only attacked after American destroyers attacked German submarines first.

2nd A Vichy French convoy of freighters and passenger ships was captured north of Madagascar by British cruisers.

3rd The British merchant ship Flynderborg was sunk off Newfoundland by German submarine U-202.

4th Viscount Halifax was pelted with eggs and tomatoes by isolationist women demonstrators in Detroit as he was leaving City Hall. Halifax was afterwards quoted as saying, "How fortunate you Americans are, in Britain we get only one egg a week and we are glad of those." The quote was actually fabricated by someone in the British Press Service, but it was widely disseminated in the media and created a burst of sympathy and goodwill towards the British and Halifax in particular.

The British battleship HMS Duke of York was commissioned.

5ᵗʰ   Isoroku Yamamoto issued Top Secret Order No. 1 to the Japanese Combined Fleet, detailing the plan for the attack on Pearl Harbour.

The Noël Coward play Blithe Spirit made its Broadway debut at the Morosco Theatre.

6ᵗʰ   Joseph Stalin made a radio address broadcast worldwide declaring that Hitler's "crazy plan" to draw Britain and the United States into a coalition to destroy the Soviet Union had failed. Stalin said that a coalition of the United States, Britain and the USSR was "now a reality" and expressed his hopes that a "second front" would be established "in the near future."

7ᵗʰ   Senior commanders of the Japanese Army and Navy were informed that the start of war against Britain and the United States was tentatively set for the 8ᵗʰ December (Japanese time).

10ᵗʰ Winston Churchill declared that although he would view "with keen sorrow" the opening of a conflict between Japan and the English-speaking world, "should the United States become involved in war with Japan the British declaration will follow within the hour."

11ᵗʰ President Roosevelt gave an Armistice Day address at Arlington National Cemetery. "Our observance of this Anniversary has a particular significance in the year 1941," the president said. "For we are able today as we were not always able in the past to measure our indebtedness to those who died ... Whatever we knew or thought we knew a few years or months ago, we know now that the danger of brutality and tyranny and slavery to freedom-loving peoples can be real and terrible. We know why these men fought to keep our freedom - and why the wars that save a people's liberties are wars worth fighting and worth winning - and at any price."

12ᵗʰ King George VI opened a new session of British Parliament. "The developments of the past year have strengthened the resolution of my peoples and of my allies to prosecute this war against aggression until final victory," his speech from the throne began.

November

13th | The British aircraft carrier Ark Royal was torpedoed and severely damaged off Gibraltar by the German submarine U-81.

14th | Despite efforts to salvage the Ark Royal, she had to be abandoned to sink some 12 hours after having been torpedoed.

15th | The Germans renewed the drive on Moscow after a three-week lull. The Soviets were pushed back from the Volga Reservoir north of the capital but with temperatures dropping to -20 Celsius across the Eastern Front, the German advance was very slow.

16th | German submarine U-433 was depth charged and sunk in the Mediterranean Sea south of Málaga by the British corvette HMS Marigold.

18th | On the 18th November 1941, the Eighth Army launched a surprise attack. The British armoured force became dispersed and suffered 530 tank losses against Axis losses of about 100 tanks up to the 22nd November. On the 23rd November the 5th South African Brigade was destroyed at Sidi Rezegh, while inflicting many German tank casualties. On the 24th November Rommel ordered the "dash to the wire", causing chaos in the British rear echelons but allowing the British armoured forces to recover. On the 27th November the New Zealanders reached the Tobruk garrison, relieving the siege. The battle continued into December, when supply shortages forced Rommel to narrow his front and shorten his lines of communication. On the 7th December 1941 Rommel withdrew the Axis forces to the Gazala position and on the 15th December ordered a withdrawal to El Agheila.

20th | Talks opened in Washington, D.C. between U.S. Secretary of State Cordell Hull, Japanese ambassador Kichisaburō Nomura and special Japanese envoy Saburō Kurusu. The Japanese demanded that the Americans withdraw from China, lift all sanctions directed against Japan and halt the U.S. naval build-up in the Pacific.

21st | Arthur Cunningham ordered the British 70th Division to break out of its encirclement at Tobruk, which it managed to do after a hard day's fighting.

November

22ⁿᵈ Operation Sunstar was a Second World War raid on Houlgate in Normandy, France over the night of the 22ⁿᵈ - 23ʳᵈ November 1941. British Commandos of No. 9 Commando took part in the raid their objective was the Batterie de Tournebride on the Butte de Houlgate. Ninety men of No.9 Commando travelled across the English Channel on HMS Prince Leopold and landed at the bottom of the Vaches Noires. The ship also transported four Assault Landing Craft which were used for the landing, four Motor Gun Boats were used to provide cover. The operation encountered difficulties and did not succeed in destroying the battery or taking any prisoners but they did obtain documents and other information.

23ʳᵈ The British 7th Armoured Division was forced to withdraw south of Sidi Rezegh after getting outflanked by Axis troops.

24ᵗʰ Gerd von Rundstedt disregarded a direct order from Hitler and withdrew from Rostov-on-Don due to Soviet counter-attacks in the rear.

25ᵗʰ The British battleship HMS Barham was torpedoed and sunk off Alexandria by German submarine U-331 with the loss of more than 800 crew.

26ᵗʰ Cordell Hull offered a counter-proposal to the Japanese demands, requiring Japan to recognize Chiang Kai-shek, withdraw from both China and French Indochina and to agree to a multinational non-aggression pact. The Japanese asked for two weeks to study the proposals.

27ᵗʰ American Admiral Husband E. Kimmel and Lieutenant General Walter Short were sent warning messages advising that negotiations with Japan had reached a stalemate and that Japan might take hostile action at any moment. The Philippines, the Kra Peninsula and Borneo were listed as among the potential sites of a Japanese attack, but Hawaii was not.

29ᵗʰ The second mass shooting of the Ninth Fort massacres occurred. A total of 4,934 German Jews were killed in the two days of shootings.

30ᵗʰ The Rumbula massacre is a collective term for incidents on the 30ᵗʰ November and the 8ᵗʰ December 1941 in which about 25,000 Jews were killed in or on the way to Rumbula forest near Riga, Latvia, during the Holocaust. Except for the Babi Yar massacre in Ukraine, this was the biggest two-day Holocaust atrocity until the operation of the death camps. About 24,000 of the victims were Latvian Jews from the Riga Ghetto and approximately 1,000 were German Jews transported to the forest by train. The Rumbula massacre was carried out by the Nazi Einsatzgruppe A with the help of local collaborators of the Arajs Kommando, with support from other such Latvian auxiliaries. In charge of the operation was Höherer SS und Polizeiführer Friedrich Jeckeln, who had previously overseen similar massacres in Ukraine.

December

1ˢᵗ The German 15th Panzer Division routed the 20th Battalion of the 2nd New Zealand Division at Belhamed, Libya, but tanks of the British 4th Armoured Brigade drove off the attack.

Japan rejected the latest U.S. proposals as "fantastic and unrealistic".

December

2nd | Japanese Rear Admiral Matome Ugaki received an order authorizing the Combined Fleet to attack any time after midnight on the 7th December, Japan time. Based on this order, Ugaki sent a wireless communication with the coded message "Climb Mount Niitaka", meaning the attacks was to go forward as planned.

3rd | The Japanese carrier fleet tasked with the Pearl Harbour attack began approaching the Hawaiian Islands with increased speed.

4th | Rainbow Five, the U.S. government's top-secret war plan, was leaked on the front pages of the Chicago Tribune and Washington Times-Herald. The plan alarmed isolationists who took it as proof that President Roosevelt was preparing to lead the United States into war against Germany, despite his pledge during the 1940 election that no Americans would be sent into foreign wars. Senator Burton K. Wheeler, without mentioning his own role in the leak, demanded a congressional investigation.

6th | President Roosevelt wrote a personal appeal to Emperor Hirohito to avoid war between the United States and Japan. "Developments are occurring in the Pacific area which threatens to deprive each of our Nations and all humanity of the beneficial influence of the long peace between our two countries." the president wrote. "Those developments contain tragic possibilities ... I address myself to Your Majesty at this moment in the fervent hope that Your Majesty may, as I am doing, give thought in this definite emergency to ways of dispelling the dark clouds. I am confident that both of us, for the sake of the peoples not only of our own great countries but for the sake of humanity in neighbouring territories, have a sacred duty to restore traditional amity and prevent further death and destruction in the world."

7th | The Japanese surprise attack on Pearl Harbour began at 7:55 a.m. Hawaiian Time. 21 American ships and over 300 aircraft were sunk or damaged and 2,418 Americans were killed. Japan lost 29 planes in return.

December

7th | Winston Churchill was dining at Chequers, the country house of the Prime Minister of the United Kingdom, with the American diplomats John Gilbert Winant and W. Averell Harriman when the news of the Pearl Harbour attack arrived. Churchill realized that the United States would now enter the war and that Britain would no longer have to fight alone. He later wrote of that night, "Being saturated and satiated with emotion and sensation, I went to bed and slept the sleep of the saved and thankful."

8th | The British House of Commons convened on short notice in light of recent events. Winston Churchill made a speech concluding, "We have at least four-fifths of the population of the globe upon our side. We are responsible for their safety and for their future. In the past we have had a light which flickered, in the present we have a light which flames, and in the future there will be a light which shines over all the land and sea."

9th | On the 9th December 1941 detachments from No. 6 and No. 12 Commandos, some Norwegian soldiers, took part in a raid on the town of Florø in Norway. Embarking on HMS Prince Charles, an infantry landing ship, they set out from Scapa Flow. During the voyage an incident occurred while some of the men were priming grenades for the raid which resulted in six men were killed and another 11 were seriously wounded, nevertheless the decision was made to continue with the raid. In the end, however, due to navigational difficulties the operation was eventually called off when the naval commander was unable to locate the fjord upon which Florø was located.

11th | Germany declared war on the United States. Hitler gave a speech to the Reichstag announcing the declaration of war.

12th | The Reich Chancellery meeting of the 12th December 1941 was held between Hitler and high-ranking officials of the Nazi Party. The meeting marked a decisive step toward the implementation of the Final Solution when Hitler announced that the Jewish race was to be annihilated.

13th | The Niihau incident ended with the death of Shigenori Nishikaichi in a struggle with people on the island and the suicide of one of his confederates, Yoshio Harada. The incident may have influenced the U.S. government's decision to intern Japanese Americans during the war, out of a belief that American citizens of Japanese ancestry might aid Japan.

15th | The British 4th Armoured Brigade arrived at Bir Halegh el Eleba where they planned to outflank the Axis forces.

16th | Hitler called on the German troops of the Eastern Front to mount "fanatical resistance" and prohibited any retreat around Moscow.

17th | Husband E. Kimmel was relieved of his command of the U.S. Pacific Fleet as part of a shake-up of officers following the Pearl Harbour attack. Kimmel was replaced by Chester Nimitz.

18th | President Roosevelt issued Executive Order 8983, appointing a commission headed by Supreme Court Justice Owen Roberts to investigate the Pearl Harbour attack in order to determine "whether any derelictions of duty or errors of judgment on the part of United States Army or Navy personnel" contributed to the success of the Japanese attack, "and if so, what these derelictions or errors were, and who were responsible therefor."

December

19th | The British destroyer Stanley was torpedoed and sunk in the Atlantic Ocean by German submarine U-574. The sloop HMS Stork then depth charged, rammed and sank U-574.

HMS Stanley   **HMS Stork**

21st | The first play of the twelve-episode radio play cycle The Man Born to Be King, based on the life of Jesus, premiered on the BBC Home Service.

22nd | The First Washington Conference, also known as the Arcadia Conference (ARCADIA was the code name used for the conference), was held in Washington, D.C., from the 22nd December 1941, to the 14th January, 1942. It brought together the top British and American military leaders in Washington,. Winston Churchill and Franklin Roosevelt and their aides had very candid conversations that led to a series of major decisions that shaped the war effort in 1942–1943. Arcadia was the first meeting on military strategy between Britain and the United States; it came two weeks after the American entry into World War II. The Arcadia Conference was a secret agreement unlike the much wider post-war plans given to the public as the Atlantic Charter, agreed between Churchill and Roosevelt in August 1941.

25th | The Battle of Hong Kong ended in Japanese victory. The Japanese occupation of Hong Kong began.

26th | British Commandos launched Operation Anklet, the raid on the Lofoten Islands.

27th | British Combined Operations executed Operation Archery, a raid against German positions on the island of Vågsøy, Norway.

30th | Winston Churchill made the "Chicken Speech" to Canadian Parliament. In reference to a comment made by Philippe Pétain that Britain would be invaded and "have its neck wrung like a chicken" by the Germans in three weeks, Churchill exclaimed, "Some chicken! Some neck!"

Soviet troops made amphibious landings in the eastern Crimea and took Kerch and Feodosia. The Germans had to stop their assault on Sevastopol in order to deal with these forces.

PEOPLE IN POWER

Robert Menzies
1939-1941
Australia
Prime Minister

Philippe Pétain
1940-1944
France
Président

Getúlio Vargas
1930-1945
Brazil
President

William Mackenzie
1935-1948
Canada
Prime Minister

Lin Sen
1931-1943
China
Government of China

Adolf Hitler
1934-1945
Germany
Führer of Germany

Marquess of Linlithgow
1936-1943
India
Viceroy of India

Benito Mussolini
1922-1943
Italy
President

Hiroito
1926-1989
Japan
Emperor

Manuel Ávila Camacho
1940-1946
Mexico
President

Joseph Stalin
1922-1952
Russia
Premier

Jan Smuts
1939-1948
South Africa
Prime Minister

Franklin D. Roosevelt
1933-1945
United States
President

Hubert Pierlot
1939-1945
Belgium
Prime Minister

Peter Fraser
1939-1949
New Zealand
Prime Minister

Sir Winston Churchill
1940-1945
United Kingdom
Prime Minister

Per Albin Hansson
1936-1946
Sweden
Prime Minister

Christian X
1912-1947
Denmark
King

Francisco Franco
1936-1975
Spain
President

Miklós Horthy
1920-1944
Hungary
Kingdom of Hungary

The Year You Were Born 1941
Book by Sapphire Publishing

Made in the USA
Las Vegas, NV
27 November 2020

11399190R00052